MANHUNT

MANHUNT

HUNTING BRITAIN'S MOST WANTED MURDERER

PETER BLEKSLEY

First published in 2020 by Ad Lib Publishers Ltd
15 Church Road
London, SW13 9HE

www.adlibpublishers.com

Text © 2020 Peter Bleksley

Paperback ISBN 978-1-913543-98-3
eBook ISBN 978-1-913543-89-1

A CIP catalogue record for this book is available from
the British Library.

Every reasonable effort has been made to trace
copyright-holders of material reproduced in this book,
but if any have been inadvertently overlooked the
publishers would be glad to hear from them.

Printed in the UK

10 9 8 7 6 5 4 3

For Liam and Lucy
I will not rest …

CONTENTS

ACKNOWLEDGEMENTS

An astonishing number of people have helped me since I launched my hunt for Kevin Parle. There are simply too many to mention individually, but you know who you are. I send you all my undying gratitude.

To everyone at Ad Lib Publishing and the BBC who have played a part in either this book or the award-winning podcast, I send you my heartfelt thanks.

To those of you who work in the media, who have granted me airtime or column inches so that I could speak about Parle and the crimes he is wanted for, I cannot thank you enough. Please be warned, I will be on the phone to you again soon.

To those who represent me, and the team, I send gratitude and apologies in equal measure.

To my long-suffering family I simply say this: I do not deserve you, but I am eternally grateful that I have you. I love you all.

And finally, to the courageous people who have reached out to tell me what you know about Parle, I remain forever indebted to each and every one of you. However, his capture still eludes me. If you know even a tiny bit more, you know what to do …

PROLOGUE

Madeleine McCann, Lord Lucan; I'm sure if I'd asked nicely enough, my publisher would have sent me out on the road, armed with my notebook and pen and my mobile phone, to research and write about either of the two biggest crime mysteries of my lifetime. But others have already done that, and I prefer to investigate cases that are no less newsworthy, yet have not garnered the publicity that I think they should have.

That's why I chose to hunt Kevin Parle. By the time you read this, I will have been hunting him for eighteen months and I will not stop until he has been found. So, if you're looking for a book with a rewarding and satisfying end, neatly tied up with a literary bow, read no further, because this true-crime story is very much ongoing – and the final chapter is yet to be written.

Liam Kelly was sixteen when he was murdered in Liverpool on 19 June 2004. He had been called to what is known in criminal circles as a 'straightener', a meeting to resolve differences. In my experience these things have a habit of turning out badly. Liam had apparently lent someone two hundred pounds and, when that money wasn't returned, he had taken it upon himself to visit the home of a relative of the man he'd lent the money to. When he didn't get what he wanted, he threw a bicycle through a window. This, apparently, was the backdrop to Liam being called on to this meeting. How pathetic, how petty, how pointless and heartbreaking is that? The events that led to his death were set in motion over nothing more than two hundred pounds.

Liam arrived in Grafton Street, Liverpool, as the passenger in a car and was approached by two men. A court was later told that the two men were Anthony Campbell and Kevin Parle. Liam apparently walked towards Campbell, then turned and walked towards Parle, who allegedly produced a shotgun and blasted the boy twice, once in the chest and once in the arm. Liam fell to the ground and dragged himself to a nearby house. He died of his injuries a short while later.

Not long after his murder, Liam's grieving mother Mary described him to the media. 'Liam was always playing on motorbikes and I was always worrying that he would have an accident. He was boyish. A proper boy. He was up to all kinds of mischief. Gorgeous Liam, the man of the house, the protector of his brothers and sisters, the son who shone.'

The police investigation into his murder moved quickly. They identified a number of suspects and made early arrests, including Parle. A young woman came forward and made an alibi statement on behalf of Parle. The police were up against a ticking clock and, unfortunately, he was bailed while the police made their inquiries into his alibi. He would never be taken into custody again.

Anthony Campbell and a man named Peter Sinclair did face court. Those present heard how Sinclair helped Parle by disposing of two mobile phones and being a lookout while Parle burned clothing that could have contained incriminating evidence. Sinclair was convicted of assisting an offender and got eight years, while Campbell was sentenced to life imprisonment for murder. The young woman who provided a false alibi statement for Parle was convicted of attempting to pervert the course of justice and received a short jail term.

On the tenth anniversary of Liam's death in June 2014, Merseyside police announced a twenty-thousand-pound reward on offer for information leading to Parle's capture, and Mary also spoke: 'Liam's murder has had a devastating effect upon the family. It has destroyed my life over the last ten years. We just want Kevin Parle brought to justice so that we can at least have some closure.'

Just over a year after Liam's murder, on 3 August 2005, on the other side of the city, Lambourne Road, Walton, in the early hours of the morning, a twenty-two-year-old mother of three young children, Lucy Hargreaves, was on the sofa in her home. Three masked men forced their way inside her home and shot her three times. Upstairs was Lucy's partner, Gary Campbell. He was in bed with their two-year-old daughter. Their other two young children were staying with their grandparents. After Lucy was shot, petrol was poured around the house and it was set ablaze. Gary Campbell and the young child escaped the blazing house by leaping out of the first-floor window.

The following year, two men, Anthony 'Fat Tony' Downes and Kirk Bradley stood trial for Lucy's murder. The prosecution presented their case, witnesses gave their testimonies and the judge ruled that the evidence was simply not strong enough, and he instructed the jury to return not guilty verdicts against the defendants. Downes and Bradley had not even had to present their defence to the charges they faced. They were duly acquitted and walked from the court as free men.

Some very capable barristers were on their team. Downes was represented by Nigel Power QC, who has a website that proudly boasts, 'Nigel represented Tony Downes when he was acquitted of the murder of Lucy Hargreaves despite compelling telephone evidence …' Clearly, that evidence was not compelling enough. I would track down another barrister who worked as part of the defence team for Downes and Bradley and who spoke on the condition of anonymity. This barrister had built a reputation for forensically examining documents, detail, facts and figures and using this in-depth analysis to dismantle prosecution cases. In the case of Downes and Bradley, he focused on mobile phone data. In 2005 courts were only just beginning to see this kind of evidence. It was a new investigative tool for the police, and they were learning as they went along.

Perhaps not surprisingly, this barrister found flaws and they were exploited by the defence. However, he told me, 'The trouble was the police made their situation worse by refusing to accept their mistakes. When such a mistake is discovered, if a police witness says, "Yep, I got that wrong, sorry," it leaves the defence barrister with nowhere to go, you have to accept their apology and move on. But in this case, they sometimes refused to do that, so it gave the defence more ammunition with which to undermine the police witnesses. They dug themselves holes which they couldn't escape from.' There may be a useful lesson there for any police officer reading this.

In the early stages of the failed court case, the jury had been told that in 1993, some twelve years before Lucy's murder, Gary Campbell, who was a teenager at the time, had been the passenger in a stolen car that was being driven around the streets of Huyton, Liverpool. The car was being treated as a plaything. Witnesses at the time told the media how the car was driven at high speed, the engine was revved excessively, and the wheels could be heard screeching as it tore around the streets. It was being driven by a fourteen-year-old called Andrew Ellis.

As Ellis reversed the car at high speed, he collided with a number of pedestrians, one of whom was four-year-old Kevin Downes. Kevin was killed instantly. Anthony 'Fat Tony' Downes was said to be traumatised by his younger brother's death. The prosecution tried to claim that the attack on Lucy's home was a revenge attack for the death of four-year-old Kevin. This remains entirely unproven.

And so to Kevin Parle. My life is dedicated to the hunt for the fugitive, for I firmly believe that the very fabric of our civilised society is based on the fundamental rule that we do not kill one another. A man who is accused of killing a sixteen-year-old boy and a twenty-two-year-old mother of three young children, in separate and horrific incidents, should not be enjoying life on the run. He should be captured so that he can be brought before a court to answer the allegations made against him.

If you feel the way that I do, then read on and let's hope that, in the not-too-distant future, Britain's most wanted man will be in handcuffs. Thank you.

Peter Bleksley, 2020

1

CONCERN

'I'm worried about you; I mean, really worried about you. These are brutal, savage crimes, committed by someone with utter disregard for life. You're my friend and I don't want anything dreadful happening to you.'

If these words had been uttered by one of those mates who works nine-to-five in an office and whose idea of danger is trying Nando's hot peri-peri sauce, then I would have been polite, appreciated their concern and dismissively replied, 'I'll be fine thanks, don't worry about me.' But here I was, sitting in the delightful garden of the country's leading criminologist, a man who has spent his entire working life dealing with vicious murderers and psychopathic serial killers. Anxiety was etched deeply across Professor David Wilson's face and for the first time in a very long while I was lost for words. David was staring at me intently. I hurriedly decided that I needed to say something that would reassure him.

'I've lived in the witness protection programme when there was a very real threat to my life and I've lived to tell the tale. I have set the parameters of my investigation to be deliberately narrow. I'm not looking to uncover and expose wider criminality. I'm merely looking for Parle.' David didn't look convinced. I burbled on, 'My home is covered by state-of-the-art CCTV. Our burglar alarm is the best that money can buy. Our steel door sits in a reinforced steel frame and I don't have a letterbox.' David's continued silence spoke volumes; he's known me long enough to know that I do not get blown off course easily. 'Look, I've been an investigator all my life. It's what I do. I find things out which certain people don't want me to know. I've got a network of open-source intelligence (OSINT) gatherers, ethical hackers and twenty-first-century digital detectives. I'm best known for tracking down pretend fugitives on *Hunted* – a bloody TV show. It makes absolute sense to me that I try to find a real one. And they don't come any more wanted than Kevin Parle.'

David took a sip of coffee and I could tell that I wasn't doing a good job of allaying his fears, so I tried a change of tack. 'Besides, I see this as public service. I'm doing something worthwhile rather than performing in an entertainment show.' David's demeanour changed in an instant, his face lit up and we went on to discuss the virtues and unparalleled satisfaction that public service can bring. With David seemingly distracted from his worries, I gave him an update on how my hunt for Parle was going and he gave me some valuable insight into the mind of someone on the run for murder.

David and I always have a hug whenever we meet or say farewell. On this occasion, he clasped me particularly tightly as I left. Not for the first time, I was heading for Liverpool.

2

WHY?

I think I must be a masochist. I always seem to set myself the most challenging of tasks when I'm looking for a project.

Researching my earlier book, *To Catch A Killer*, had thrown up all sorts of difficulties, not the least of them being that I was refused cooperation by the police, the murder victim's wife and the bank that he worked for. Any sane writer would have canned the idea and moved on to an easier subject. But those refusals merely served as red rags to this rather determined bull and I ploughed ahead, made numerous expensive trips to Scotland, developed a number of trusted and reliable sources and got the book written. Along the way I achieved the three main goals that I set myself, each of which apply to the book you're reading now.

Firstly, I have to drum up significant publicity for the case. Airtime and column inches are the aim, because they raise awareness and that encourages people to come forward and tell me what they know. If you search online for Alistair Wilson, who was the murder victim discussed in *To Catch A Killer*, you will come across my name, for I was very successful in getting on the telly, on the radio and in the papers.

Secondly, by achieving my first goal I send a very clear message to my subject: I'm on their case and I will not give up. Alistair Wilson's killer knows that and should not rest easily in his bed, for information continues to come my way. Likewise, the subject of this book, Kevin Parle, undoubtedly knows that I'm coming for him, and I'm sure my efforts in the past eighteen months have caused him some considerable discomfort and inconvenience. Good. I'm not about to stop hunting him any time soon. This book is the next step on my journey towards finding him. You are reading the longest 'wanted poster' ever, for which I am very grateful. When you're done reading, please leave this book on the sunlounger you're relaxing on, or the plane or train you're travelling on, or lend it to a family member or friend. Spread the word, show the pictures, and together let's make Kevin Parle the most well-known fugitive on the planet.

Finally, I have to put previously unknown information into the public domain. Sharing what I've discovered may just encourage the person who holds the last piece of the jigsaw to come forward, because they may think, This bloke actually knows his stuff, he's got off his backside to do some proper research, so I'll talk to him.

In recent years I have spent many days in the company of those who have lost a loved one to murder and never seen anyone brought to justice for those crimes. Their pain does not go away. They find a way to manage it, but it is there, gnawing away in its own corrosive way; for justice is central to our very existence and when we feel something is unjust, it hurts. I'm not naïve. I know only too well that our world is far from perfect, that justice does not always reign. I've stood outside the Old Bailey, watching a bunch of crooks who I knew were bang to rights, laughing, joking and giving me a two-fingered salute as they pranced off to the nearest pub to celebrate the fact that they had got off. Shit happens.

But justice and our belief that it will prevail remains central to our thinking. Or else we might as well all take up arms and summarily dispense our own vigilante-style punishment to anybody we think deserves it. And then where would we be?

3

THE BUILD-UP

The date of my press conference was Monday 29 April, 2019, but the work had begun many weeks before then.

I'd researched Kevin Parle and the crimes he was wanted for from the comfort of my box bedroom office. I'd read just about every article ever written about him and had submitted a synopsis to my publishers. These stalwarts of the literary world liked the idea of my manhunt and didn't mind taking a calculated risk. There was a possibility that Parle could be captured before I'd even written this book, which would mean the whole project would have to be delayed to avoid prejudicing the outcome of any criminal trial, but they were willing to take a punt.

Researching unsolved murders and hunting down fugitives is an expensive business, especially when the crimes involved are many hundreds of miles from my home. The advance from my publishers was by no means huge and has had to cover travel, accommodation and living expenses. It has not been anywhere near enough to cover my costs, so I have to take on other work to fund my investigations. That's why you may see me popping up on *Good Morning Britain*, the *Jeremy Vine* show, or making a complete fool of myself on shows like *Britain's Got More Talent*. It's why I do public-speaking gigs. It's all about putting cash in my investigations pot and attracting more attention to the case.

To further boost my chances of capturing my target, I decided to make a public launch of my hunt for Parle at a press conference in Liverpool, out of respect to that great city, its people and the murder victims who lived there, Liam Kelly and Lucy Hargreaves. I was decidedly nervous because I was still not sure if there would be any interest in me and my hunt.

I notified Merseyside police of my intentions, as past experience had taught me that some police forces regarded me as a nuisance. A mate of mine had recently attended a social function in Scotland with senior police officers in attendance. He overheard a senior officer talking about the Alistair Wilson case: 'We thought we'd done a reasonable job on that investigation, until that irritating c**t Peter Bleksley showed up, poking his fucking nose around and causing us a shitload more work.' I had mixed feelings about this. I was glad that my revelations had caused the force to do more work. I knew their investigation had been flawed, but I was disappointed that they held such a narrow-minded, unimaginative view of what I do. It had always been my intention to work with police in Scotland, but they wanted a one-way street – their idea was I would tell them everything and they would gave me nothing in return. I don't know of a relationship on Earth that works well that way.

I was hoping for a more enlightened attitude from the police in Liverpool. I went to the very top. I emailed Chief Constable Andy Cooke an outline of my intentions and ambitions. I made it clear that I was not setting out to embarrass the police in any way, but that I hoped we all shared the same goal, that of capturing Kevin Parle. I also attached a copy of my book synopsis. I could not have been more open or transparent.

Somebody within Merseyside police knew me already, from the hunt for an escaped prisoner. In 2014, Shaun Walmsley had murdered thirty-three-year-old Anthony Duffy in a dispute over drugs. Walmsley was sentenced to life imprisonment with a minimum term of thirty years. In 2016, he made an appeal that failed and knew he would be in his late fifties by the time he became eligible for parole. Clearly not thrilled at the prospect, Walmsley and associates staged a successful armed escape during a hospital visit. In February 2018, while I was still the chief of Channel 4's *Hunted*, Merseyside police tweeted out, 'Peter Bleksley, can you help support our appeal? Shaun Walmsley is a highly dangerous individual convicted of a savage murder. We are determined to find him.' They wanted me to retweet their message and I added, 'Only too happy to help. Where's Walmsley? You can contact me in absolute confidence. I can guarantee lifelong anonymity.'

I'm not sure if the police were thrilled at me offering lifelong anonymity to anybody that came forward, but that was the deal I put on the table and I meant it. I had previous in this regard. I once gave evidence in a case in which I had worked undercover, and it got to a very tricky point in the trial where the judge ordered me to disclose the identity of the person who had introduced me as a fellow crook to the defendants. As far as I was concerned this was a wholly unjustified fishing exercise by a smart defence barrister and I refused. The judge did his nut and threatened me with all sorts, but I held firm. He had already put me in danger by forcing me to give evidence using my real name rather than my undercover identity; he and I were not exactly on friendly terms.

After days of legal arguments and ferocious cross-examination by barristers and the judge, it came to the crunch. Either I revealed the identity or the case would be slung out. So be it. I was not going to bow to threats and intimidation, wherever it came from. To the sound of cheering and clapping from the dock and the public gallery, the defendants were set free, and the judge summonsed me back into the witness box. He completely lost his rag and told me that I was in contempt of court. Fuck him. He then bottled out of sending me to prison, saying it should be a matter for the director of public prosecutions. He released me, pending that decision. I walked from the court in time to see the defendants and their friends and family firmly sticking it to the officer in the case. As I joined this beleaguered detective inspector, the south London, old-time lag that I had spent a lot of time negotiating with in my undercover guise hollered over, 'Oi, Detective Inspector, that Peter Bleksley is a lot better man than your informants. At least he keeps his mouth shut.' In my life, the rules I abided by then stand firm today: I do not declare my sources, unless of course you choose to double-cross me, in which case all bets are off.

In 2018, the *Liverpool Echo* ran a story mentioning me, headlined, MERSEYSIDE POLICE ASK REALITY TV DETECTIVE FOR HELP IN HUNT FOR SHAUN WALMSLEY. They described me as tough-talking. I thought there was more than a hint of sarcasm in the final line of their article: 'Officers would ask anybody, reality TV or otherwise, who has seen Walmsley, to contact them …' The fugitive was finally captured by armed police in Leeds. He apparently said to the police, as they bundled him, handcuffed, into the back of a car, 'Good job, boys.'

Now I was letting the same police force know about my new case. I didn't have to wait long for a reply. I was soon talking to the man in charge of the police hunt for Parle, a detective chief inspector (DCI), who will remain nameless. I had some additional news for him.

4

THE LAUNCH

In 2018 *Celebrity Hunted* was nominated for a BAFTA and my beloved mate Ben Owen – my deputy on the show and later chief – and I put on our posh togs for the ceremony. By and large the evening was a complete pile of old tosh. We got beaten in our category by *Love Island*, which didn't help the evening.

We had first been crammed together in a reception area where a young lady, who had clearly had a very early start to her drinking, managed to puke all over my shoes at 6.30 p.m. But there was one notable highlight that evening. While outside for a smoke, I met a giant of a man who introduced himself as Mark. It didn't take long for me to discover that he was a podcast producer with an interest in true crime. That was it, we were off and running, the conversation and questions were non-stop. Mark and I exchanged phone numbers before we parted and vowed to meet again over another smoke. We did exactly that, when we discovered instant chemistry and agreed it would be great if we could work together on a podcast some time. Mark made the potential of a series feel like a very different proposition from the slow and frustrating processes involved in TV production. He thought it was likely to get commissioned because there was a lot less money involved in the making of a podcast, explaining that it would just be him and a microphone accompanying me. There would be some money to put towards the hunt which would be great, because I was convinced there would be some foreign travel involved in this case.

Mark went off and pitched the idea to the BBC and arranged a meeting with a couple of their senior radio people. Over a coffee a few months later, I very enthusiastically explained what I was going to do and how I would do it. We were asked to make a pilot episode of *Manhunt: Finding Kevin Parle*, and now it seemed a number of ducks were beginning to fall into a rather neat row.

Ahead of the press conference there was a lot to get done: a website had to be built, the invitations had to be sent out and I got hundreds of flyers printed. I wanted large posters of Parle printed. As the day of the conference loomed, I tallied up the expense so far: £1,800 out of pocket already. Don't tell the wife.

I had a long telephone chat with the DCI from Merseyside police. He was the epitome of professionalism and extremely courteous. We agreed that we shared the aim of seeing Parle captured but the DCI, however, was now dealing with an unprecedented situation – capturing fugitives was for law enforcement, not for writers. Over various conversations, we agreed we had the interests of the victim's families at heart. Sixteen-year-old Liam Kelly and twenty-two-year-old Lucy Hargreaves, those young lives cut brutally short, motivated us, always. The DCI informed the families about my work, but they told him they were not willing to speak to me at this stage. Of course, I was disappointed, but I harboured the hope that they might change their minds once they saw what I was doing and the progress I hoped to make. Mark also hoped to interview Liam and Lucy's relatives. He was determined to put Liam and Lucy at the very front of the podcast series, and rightly so.

I did wonder if I should adopt a rather cynical attitude and convince myself that the police had told them not to speak to me, but I have no evidence of that. Even so, if that had happened it wouldn't have surprised me because the police's natural default position is that of control, it's what they do. The police control crowds at football matches or demonstrations. They control victims, witnesses, investigations, suspects, one another; control is what they do and, in my experience, when they are not in control, they don't like it. I've known many cops who finish work only to go home and control their partners. Maybe that's part of the reason why so many of them get divorced.

Anyway, the DCI couldn't control me, and I think he was wise enough to recognise that. He gave me the impression of being a thoroughly decent bloke, who I suspected might be a bit of fun once he's off-duty, freed of the shackles of rank, position and procedure.

One of the questions I was very keen to get an answer to was whether or not the twenty-thousand-pound reward that had previously been on offer for information leading to Parle's capture still stood. That was a very tempting carrot to dangle and I was keen to make that known far and wide. The DCI confirmed its existence, but said it was subject to Parle's capture and conviction. I felt this was manifestly unfair on any public-spirited citizen who gave the vital information only to see the cash disappear if Parle was later found not guilty: there are so many factors that affect a criminal trial. The police can make a mistake during their investigation.

The Crown Prosecution Service can get something wrong, perhaps failing to disclose relevant information to the defence that can cause a case to collapse. A judge can misdirect a jury. A jury can be nobbled by criminals who find out where the jurors live and threaten then. And sometimes juries just return perverse verdicts. There are many more reasons why a person can be acquitted, not least because they're innocent.

What if Parle was caught and found guilty of one murder but not the other? Was the DCI seriously saying the reward would not be paid even under those circumstances? That would be utterly preposterous. The DCI said that the police would have to take a pragmatic view. Too bloody right they would, I thought to myself. I was not particularly happy, but our discussions always remained polite and courteous, despite any differing views. The DCI took the news of a possible BBC podcast series in addition to the book in his stride.

The press conference was held in London in the end, rather than Liverpool. It was felt that some key journalists wouldn't make the journey up north. I've given hundreds of media interviews over the years, but as my agent and the team began setting up the banners, posters and flyers, the nerves started to jangle. Mark arrived in good time, complete with his microphone, of course. I was waiting for the news outlets, the big hitters who would guarantee that my hunt for Parle was heard. I was delighted to see Danny Shaw, the BBC home affairs correspondent. The Press Association were also present and as many media outlets took a feed from their output, this was a result.

I told the assembled journalists why I was going to hunt Parle and what my motives were. I have absolutely no idea how long I spoke for because I was so engrossed. There was a stream of relevant, well-placed questions, which I felt I handled OK. Mark, my agent and I all thought it had gone well, that the number and range of journos present was good and that the hunt had got off to a positive start.

I hailed a black cab and dragged in my small but very heavy suitcase, containing the many hundreds of flyers I was going to distribute in Liverpool. I also had a rucksack that was so full I could barely close the zips, and a large cardboard tube containing the rolled-up Kevin Parle posters. I may have uttered the odd expletive as I bundled all this stuff into the cab. My destination was the still young radio station talkRADIO and Eamonn Holmes, who I have known for years. Back in the day, when he was presenting the breakfast show on Sky News, I'd quite often be alongside him talking about crime and policing. Now he was presenting the drive-time show and allowing me to spread the word about Parle.

Normally, I pride myself on being professional in studios – I leave my phone outside, switched to silent or in airplane mode. I now had a burner phone that I'd sourced purely to use in my hunt for Parle. Its number was on the flyers, posters and banners and had been given to the journos who'd attended the press conference. I'm looking at that phone as I type this now. It is always within my reach. In my wildest and nonsensical dreams I hoped that, soon after going public with my hunt, somebody would call me with the vital information on Parle's whereabouts. You can guess the next bit, right? Yep, you got it, as I was broadcasting to the nation the blooming thing rang. I was embarrassed and excited in equal measure. The excitement soon disappeared once I discovered the caller was a lazy journalist who couldn't be arsed to dig out my personal phone number. I hurriedly apologised and explained to the listeners why I had the phone. Affable Eamonn was absolutely fine with it. We talked about the details of the murders Parle was wanted for and what I had already discovered about him.

It was soon time for another expensive black cab journey, this time to Euston station to catch a train to Liverpool. I was laden down with all my clobber and I didn't fancy trudging up and down escalators and battling onto trains. I met up with Mark again at Euston and we discussed strategy over a hurriedly demolished plate of pasta.

I was spreading the word about my hunt for Parle before I even reached my destination. A British Transport Police officer recognised me from TV and we started to chat. His dedication to his role as a police officer shone through. I know our world is a far from perfect one and the same can be said of our police, but in my considerable experience the overwhelming majority of our front-line officers are dedicated public servants to whom we owe a great debt. Sadly, they are often led by fools in the very senior ranks. In the past decade policing has largely been devalued, dismantled and nearly destroyed, particularly by Theresa May. Thank fuck she's no longer in the Home Office or Downing Street, because she's a deluded and dangerous idiot. Our brave police officers became demoralised beyond compare because of her failure to understand or appreciate modern-day policing and the savage cuts she imposed on policing budgets that led to some twenty thousand fewer police patrolling the streets. I sincerely hope policing is repaired by politicians, and soon. We are all in a bit more danger if it is not.

Another delightful passenger was convinced she recognised me from *Dragon's Den*. I bloody wish! My small pile of fivers would look distinctly out of place alongside the wads of fifty-pound notes that the multi-millionaire Dragons have on display in the show. I politely pointed out where she might have seen me instead and, of course, she also received a flyer.

Two hours flew by and Liverpool Lime Street station was almost in view. I was returning to a city with which I had quite a bit of history. I wanted to be the first off so that I could position myself by the ticket barriers and hand out flyers to our fellow passengers as they headed for the exit. Mark and I struggled through numerous train carriages, taking great care not to bash anyone with our bags of clothing and kit, as we made our way to the front of the train. A tip – when you hand out flyers, make sure you tell people that you're not trying to sell them anything. Explain as quickly as you can who you are and what you're doing. Some people will always blank you, others may take a flyer and quickly discard it, but I didn't have to wait long before I had a bit of a result.

One family were happy to talk. The mum claimed to be the cousin of a famous Liverpool football legend. She instantly knew who Parle was and expressed her disgust at the crimes he was wanted for and the fact that he was still on the run. She gave me a second- or third-hand story of how Parle was seen to bottle someone in a hotel bar in Spain. The assault she described was vicious and apparently without motive but, unfortunately for me, she had not witnessed the crime herself. The man explained that the hotel was frequented by prostitutes, to which his daughter exclaimed, 'How do you know that, Dad?' We all laughed as her dad squirmed, explaining that it was just one of those things he knew.

Mark said we thought Parle had run with a notorious firm of Liverpool fans who called themselves the Urchins. The dad took a sharp intake of breath and stepped back at the mere mention of this gang. 'Everyone knows the Urchins,' he said with more than a hint of fear in his voice. The family wished me good luck with my search and promised to spread the word. I thought this was a very encouraging start to our time in Liverpool, although their hotel story had been a bit light on detail and they didn't know its exact location. I wasn't able to put any flesh on the bones of this tale, nor have I been able to find any evidence whatsoever that Parle committed that particular assault. However, first-hand accounts of Parle and his unpleasantness would not be long in coming.

Another lady we spoke to at the railway station suggested Parle might be in Holland, but she said that was just her theory, largely based upon the fact that two other notorious criminals from Liverpool, Anthony 'Fat Tony' Downes and Kirk Bradley, who had both been acquitted of Lucy's murder, had been captured there for other offences some years ago. You'll hear more of them later, as well.

Mark and I jumped into a cab and asked the driver to take us to the budget hotel I'd used a few months earlier when I'd delivered a talk about my research work. The rooms were clean, had a comfy bed, a shower and there was a bar. It was perfect for my needs. By the time we'd dumped our bags it was 9.30 p.m.

I find it very helpful to talk to publicans and cab drivers. They tend to know their city or town and what's going on because they interact with the public all the time: they have their ears to the ground. I asked the hotel receptionist to direct us to the nearest pub and, ten minutes later, Mark and I had pints of delicious bitter in one hand and bunches of flyers in the other. I asked the landlord if it was OK to hand out flyers to his punters. He was fine with that. In fact, he took a read of my flyer and asked a few questions about the murders. Then Mark headed to one end of the bar and I started at the other. We were both surprised by the reaction we got from the customers. Universally, it was, 'Kevin who? No, never heard of him.' We spent considerable time explaining the murders and what I was doing. But the punters came on board and all asked if they could take more than one flyer to show to family, friends or work colleagues. I was massively encouraged by these responses.

It had been a long, full-on day as Mark and I left the pub and wearily made our way back to the hotel. By way of a nightcap we bought a bottle of wine from the hotel bar which we drank on a terrace out the back that overlooked the renovated docks. Our journey into the unknown was now well and truly underway. There was no turning back, no shelving the book idea or ditching the podcast in favour of doing something easier or better paid. Through my press conference, my posts on social media and my interactions with the public, the word was unmistakably out there. Many people now knew I was hunting Kevin Parle.

5

THE FIRST OF MANY

It was 7.10 a.m. on day two of my search and I was unusually enjoying a deep slumber in my hotel bed. I'm normally an early riser. I heard an unfamiliar ringing noise which I struggled to recognise for a few moments. Then it dawned on me it was my burner phone.

I am hyper-sensitive to my regular phone's ringtone. The phone is usually with me twenty-four hours a day. I sometimes find myself reaching out to answer it, only to realise it's an advert or TV drama. If only I could figure out how to download some personalised, fancy ringtone then I suppose that wouldn't happen. Mind you, whenever I hear someone answer to the theme tune from *The Sweeney* or some football chant, I don't exactly think of the owner in glowing terms.

As soon as I realised what was calling me, I leaped straight out of bed in complete panic mode, grabbed at the phone, fumbled it for what seemed like an eternity before eventually finding the right button to answer. I was hugely relieved when I heard a voice at the other end; I had been worried they would have hung up. This caller cut straight to the point. He told me that he had seen a man who he believed was

Kevin Parle only ten days earlier, at a travelling funfair in a town called Hilversum, Holland. The caller explained that he was an expat Liverpudlian and that he had followed the police hunt for Parle in the media over the years. He had also caught the early publicity around my search and decided to pass this information on. This caller was very precise with the date, time and location of this sighting. He went on to tell me there was a permanently sited CCTV camera at the entrance to the funfair, which would have definitely filmed the man he thought was Parle. The source told me he had felt quite intimated when he had walked past the man because he was convinced he'd just had a close encounter with a man wanted for two murders. The source told me I could call him back if need be but only at specific times. I thanked him, leaned back in my chair and pondered what to do next.

I was gagging for a cup of coffee and a fag. I can't begin to function properly in the morning until I've had caffeine and nicotine (I don't expect to make old bones – if I do it'll be some kind of miracle). I threw a pair of jeans over my pyjama bottoms, pulled on a fleece and made my way downstairs. I fed my cravings and was considerably more awake than I had been when the burner phone first rang. I returned to look at my scribbled notes and cursed myself out loud. There were some gaps in the information, some questions that I should have asked the caller but didn't. I was pretty pissed off with myself. I began to question whether I was really up to the task I'd set myself. At fifty-nine years old, was the brain too old and slow for the cut and thrust of hunting someone like Parle? I sat in silence for a few moments. I parked my self-doubt firmly elsewhere. 'I will do this,' my brain shouted to itself.

Due to the time restraints the source had imposed, I knew we wouldn't be able to speak for another twenty-four hours, but as the information was so recent I felt it needed an urgent response. I was going to be in Liverpool for another three days. Whoever operated that CCTV system in Holland was highly unlikely to allow me access to the footage as a writer, and most definitely not a part of the establishment. Time was of the essence, I thought, but I really needed to consider my next move. If I was going to pass on to the police every scrap of information I received, then I would be nothing more than their stooge and I think the media and the public would quickly suss that out. Any credibility I had as an investigative writer would go straight out of the window. Sources would not come forward and confide in me. I had to retain some sense of independence. I strongly suspected that the relationship I was going to have with the police was anyway going to be another one-way street, as it had been in Scotland. The Merseyside DCI had termed our relationship 'informal', which was pretty vague, to say the least.

In the end, I came to the conclusion that I didn't really have a choice, because this sighting needed a dynamic response. I passed the information on to the DCI. I apologised to him for the gaps in the information and promised to rectify those when I spoke to the caller the following day. The DCI chuckled when I explained that I hadn't been at my sharpest first thing in the morning, especially after a very long day the day before and half a bottle of wine as a nightcap. I liked the fact he had a sense of humour.

The media in Liverpool were extremely interested in what I was doing, including the *Liverpool Echo*, BBC regional radio and television and Granada, the regional TV station. Some came to the hotel, which was handy, while others wanted us to go to them, which I was only too happy to do. I am very fortunate to have 'minor celebrity' status because it opens doors and gets me the press coverage I need. I was also lucky to have Mark with me. Not only was he fielding many of the calls from the media, but he'd hired a car and was only too willing to drive me around. We were getting so much more done than I'd managed when I'd previously been on my own. He also took his microphone everywhere to record what I was doing, in the hope of gathering enough quality material to convince the BBC to commission the podcast series.

Mark, as an enormous bonus, is a really lovely man. We have many common interests, including football and cricket. He's West Ham and Essex, I'm QPR and Kent, leading to some lively exchanges. We're of a similar age, although he occasionally reminds me he's the marginally younger one. We both have teenage sons and strong-minded wives. Our sense of humour is strikingly similar and we both laugh at ourselves a lot. He's a vastly experienced journalist, a background that blends well with my investigative career. We both like a drink. He's the perfect work colleague for me, and quite frankly, I adore him.

The hotel manager was very accommodating and allowed us to record some interviews in the restaurant. This involved camera crews shifting around a lot of furniture, but he didn't mind in the slightest. His cooperation, and that of his staff, coupled with the inexpensive and delicious red wine they stocked, guaranteed my business on many of the subsequent trips we made to Liverpool. I held numerous meetings there with those who were helping me in my hunt. The manager followed my hunt for Parle, even when we hadn't stayed in his hotel for some months, and later wished me all the best for the future.

One of my meetings over the next couple of days was with a couple of former colleagues, one of whom has a wide network of open-source intelligence experts. These are devilishly clever people who can legitimately and legally search the very deepest, darkest corners of the internet, finding stuff out about all of us that we don't even realise is out there. But you have to know how and where to look, and have the right software tools. They don't just turn up material through a simple Google search.

This former colleague also has an army of 'ethical hackers', invariably young people, who test the capabilities of corporate IT systems, security infrastructure and more, looking for the vulnerabilities that criminals may seek to exploit and advising their clients accordingly. And they were willing to come on board my hunt. As one of my former colleagues said, 'If Parle's alive, he's online'. He also went on to suggest that the fugitive would have made multiple enemies while he was on the run, and one of them might possess the information I needed.

Another person present at this meeting, Liverpool born and raised, went on to explain that a large number of Irish, Welsh, Scandinavian and other nationalities that are seen as being anti-authoritarian, have settled in Liverpool over the years. Consequently, an anti-establishment mindset often prevails in the city. He thought I was going to have a very difficult time getting people to engage with me because, as an ex-cop, they might still regard me as an authority figure. I needed to prove him wrong.

We had a long conversation about whether Parle was dead or not. Some people had started messaging me on the burner phone, using rather unpleasant language. Others chose to insult me on Twitter or Facebook. Many of them were saying that Parle was dead, and that I'd need a deep-sea diving suit to find him, or that he'd been chopped into bits and thrown in the Mediterranean. This was clearly a line of thinking that a considerable number of people in Liverpool chose to follow. A quick perusal of the public comments posted below articles about me and Parle that appeared in the *Liverpool Echo* bore this out. I could completely understand why. I firmly believe that the overwhelming majority of us believe in justice, we want to see justice handed down, and for some, the thought of Parle being dead brings them some kind of closure, and I get that way of thinking. The trouble was that there was not one shred of evidence to support that theory. His body had never been found, no shallow grave, no charred remains, no body parts, no bloodstained crime scene had ever been discovered, all there was to support this theory were urban myths.

It was also a very convenient rumour to have swirling around if you were Kevin Parle. It might distract, demotivate or demoralise anyone looking for you. I fully appreciated that, after some fourteen years, the police might have current murder enquiries that they needed to solve and other fugitives to find; I didn't expect after all these years for there to be a huge team of detectives dedicated to Parle. That was part of my reasoning behind launching my hunt.

As the meeting drew to a close, we all agreed that, had criminals killed Parle, they would have wanted people to know about it, and would have deliberately left his body somewhere where it could be found. They would have used some clear and distinctive sign, like leaving his head in a bag to be discovered by a passerby. The aim would have been to spread fear and terror, so that people would have been intimidated. In the absence of any such evidence, I was going to work on the theory that Parle was very much alive. If I did discover that he was dead somewhere along the line, then I felt I would have also done my job, although my heartfelt hope was to find Kevin Parle alive.

The media interviews continued, and in some of these I adopted a robust tone towards those that were insulting me and telling me Parle was dead. I said that I had a shovel in the boot of my car to dig up any grave, that I would travel to any corner of the world if need be, and basically, they had to put up or shut up. If he was dead, prove it.

There has never been any proof of his death forthcoming but, for the first time in my years of investigating in the public arena, I was beginning to attract abuse. Invariably, it was from cowardly keyboard-warriors, who would set up an account on social media such as Twitter, Facebook or LinkedIn and begin to troll and attempt to taunt me. I say attempt, because I really am not going to be in the slightest bit bothered by some faceless, nameless coward who doesn't have the courage to show their face or give their real name. Some of the abuse I got was laughable, some of the taunting was pitiful, and some was abusive. The culprits are pathetic vermin who I'm sure would run a mile in the face of danger in real life. One of these cretins posted a picture of my house on Twitter, together with my address and an accurate description of the bedroom I sleep in. I say to them, congratulations, Sherlock, for a career best bit of detective work. Quite what they thought they were going to achieve I don't know. Anyone who knows me knows that I am not the sort of person to be cowed by such nonsense, nor will I be terrified into stopping what I set out to achieve. Were friends or associates of Parle behind these online assaults? Who knows? One such twat who spewed poisonous bile about me claimed to be an ex-police officer.

Fake accounts were also set up in my name, and in Parle's name. Some were set up by such morons that all they could manage by the way of inventiveness was to spell the word Parle backwards. It makes you wonder what kind of imbecile sits around with nothing better to do than waste their time doing this kind of crap. I suspect they probably have one hand on the keyboard and one hand on their tiny penises when they do this. I had to get the accounts in my name taken down for impersonation and other misdemeanours. It must irk those who posted reputation-damaging stuff to know that I've never been busier or more in demand for work since they wrote garbage about me online. Thank you, trolls.

Should you ever encounter similar characters, please ignore them. Do not rise to their pathetic bait. Take a deep breath and walk away, and whatever you do, do not engage with them. I learnt the hard way, because in the early days of being trolled I fought back and engaged with them. That is one very big mistake. Recognition of any description is what they crave, so even when you show them up for being the arseholes that they are or destroy them with sharper wit and intellect, they still get off on it. A response of any description provides them with the oxygen of venom on which they survive. Please, just don't feed the trolls. Of course, you should block or mute or report them, just do not respond. Force them to get their kicks elsewhere.

6

DOES HE KNOW?

This first trip to Liverpool was turning out very well. A considerable number of people were getting in touch and I had some clandestine meetings with certain contacts, far from their home areas, to ensure no prying eyes were able to connect them with me and Mark. Everywhere we went Mark had his microphone at the ready and, even though I was only a couple of days into this project, the people we met were truly inspiring. Through all the meetings, one thing shone through and that was the type of man we were up against. The majority said words to the effect of, 'Parle is a smart guy, an intelligent man, whatever you do, do not underestimate him.'

I couldn't help wondering if Parle was aware of all the press coverage. And not for the first time, that got me thinking about what he was doing now. Wherever he may be, was he going to be sitting tight and hoping that it would all blow over? I decided that I might drive myself round the bend if I focused on that too often, and for too long, but I was contemplating whether he had a strategy for dealing with the increased awareness that people would now have about his name and the crimes he was wanted for.

Mark and I sat by the river one night, having a drink and mulling over what we'd done that day and we had a fabulous view over the renovated docks of Liverpool as we pondered, theorised and planned our next move. My existing affection for this great city was deepening. I was not the only member of my family with a love of this place. My eldest son studied at John Moores University in Liverpool. He had been born in 1988, the result of an on-off relationship that suffered from challenges that were the result of my work as a detective: I had inadvertently ended up being part of a team that was involved in the arrest of my girlfriend's brother and had to contribute to the subsequent, tortuous court case. Not surprisingly, perhaps, this scenario placed huge pressures on our relationship but, from the moment my girlfriend told me she was pregnant, I vowed that I would always be there for our baby, even though my relationship with his mum was not to last. I am proud to say I have been true to my word and, over the past thirty-two years my adorable son and I have enjoyed a very close relationship that has been overwhelmingly joyous and brimming with boundless love.

On his first day at the university in Liverpool, I drove him to his digs, my car laden down with all his stuff. Once I'd lugged most of his clobber up to his new student flat, and he had excitedly met his new mates, he couldn't get me out of there quick enough. I hugged him, but not for too long, because his new pals were watching, planted a kiss on his cheek and disappeared. Tears were welling up in my eyes before I'd reached my car. I somehow managed to steer it around a couple of side streets before parking up and howling like a baby. I gathered myself together after a couple of minutes; this was all about a new adventure for him, and not about how much I would miss him.

He fell in love with Liverpool very quickly, and it is a love that has simply never left him. He returns to hook up with his old uni friends whenever he can. And while he was studying, I made many trips to see him, when he would show me around the city, take me to his favourite haunts – which were so often pubs – and introduce me to his fellow students. Those trips used to cost me a fortune as I couldn't bring myself to accept a drink from a student. I lost count of the rounds I bought. He stayed in Liverpool after graduating and if he'd managed to find the job that he really wanted at the time, I reckon he would have stayed and really put down some roots. My times with him in Liverpool were wonderful and I cherish those memories. I gained a clear insight into why he adored the city, and consequently my affection for the place and its people was strong.

7

LIAM AND LUCY

I met a private investigator in Liverpool with decades of experience who was convinced that Parle would be close to home – that he wouldn't have ventured very far.

I was keeping an open mind on this but we'd already learnt that Parle was not only a big man, six-foot six-inches tall and broadly built, but that he was a large character, and liked to play the big man, to show off. I thought that in his arrogance might lie his vulnerability. But it was becoming very clear that I was going to need a considerable number of people to help me on top of the investigators, the open source intelligence experts, ethical hackers and the like. I was going to need not only an army of the public to be my eyes and ears, but also criminals, because in all likelihood it was them who would be helping Parle every step of the way.

Another investigator I met was very used to pushing boundaries both legally and ethically, and we had a conversation about tactics. She asked me if I was going to put fake news out in an effort to unnerve Parle, throw him off his stride and force him into making an error. Her attitude was very much, 'It's better to ask for forgiveness than it is for permission.' I can understand there may be circumstances in which that rule might be very apt, but if the BBC were going to commission the podcast, I would have to act with integrity and behave ethically at all times. I wasn't going to break the law by, for example, illegally accessing data, or hacking into someone's phone, because, quite frankly, I didn't want to get nicked. And I need to occupy the moral high ground. I made a firm commitment to operate within the law throughout my hunt for Parle. I'd think creatively and do stuff the police can't, but there would be no point in seeing Parle in a police cell, only for me to be in the one next to him.

Mark and I made our way to Grafton Street in the Dingle part of Liverpool, where sixteen-year-old Liam Kelly was brutally murdered in the early hours of Saturday 19 June, 2004. We didn't meet anyone who described Liam as a model student, and it's fair to say he was a bit of a likely lad. Others described him in far more disparaging terms. But he was only a teen, a boy, denied the chance to grow, to mature, to enter manhood and find a partner, start a family and then settle down and provide for them. He was not to have any of that and it angers me, a lot.

We met some fantastic people in Grafton Street. They were aware of what I was doing. They were only too happy to talk to us and they told us how one of Liam's relatives still comes to Grafton Street every year on Liam's birthday and that he ties flowers to the railings on the opposite side of the road from where Liam fell. Apparently, this relative always sits for a few hours, remembering, thinking and pondering. We met another neighbour who said they take refreshments out to the relative and always have a chat with him. There was still a strong feeling amongst the residents of Grafton Street that we met, and who had lived there at the time of

Liam's murder that, while some people had been arrested and convicted, there was very much unfinished business because Parle was still at large.

Mark and I stayed in Grafton Street for a couple of hours, talking to residents about the area, which is essentially row upon row of terraced houses. Most of them are beautifully kept and the street was clean and tidy. There was obviously a huge sense of pride felt by many residents. I vowed that I would be back.

We made our way to Lambourne Road, on the other side of the city, about half-an-hour's drive from Grafton Street, in Walton. It was here on, 3 August 2005, that another murder took place, of twenty-two-year-old Lucy Hargreaves. Three masked men gained entry and she was shot twice. Mark and I were received as warmly as we had been in Grafton Street. People were keen to tell us about the impact of Lucy's murder, one that was still felt in the neighbourhood. They were happy for Mark to record their voices. Apparently, at the time of the killing, Lambourne Road had been quite run-down, but since then money had been invested and the homes, overwhelmingly, looked presentable. There was again a tangible sense of injustice because nobody had ever been convicted in connection with Lucy's brutal murder.

Many residents told us that folk in Liverpool do not grass on one another. They explained that this was the Scouse mindset. And when it comes to authority? 'We don't talk to them. That's just how it is.' However, a few people told us that they felt the senseless and merciless slaughter of a beautiful twenty-two-year-old woman crossed the line and they said, 'If we knew anything, we'd tell you.' The next few months were to reveal that quite a few people did know things that they were willing to tell me.

8

INSIGHT

I got a phone call from a person who told us they could give us a lot of background information about the Parle family, including Kevin, of course, and this contact was very happy to meet.

They chose the location, a very decent pub far away from Liverpool. We spent a couple of hours getting a real insight into the Parles, some of which was very relevant. When I asked this source what Parle was like as a youngster the immediate response was, 'He was a little shit, he was always scrapping.' Parle's mum, Shirley, was described as a lovely woman; hard-working, salt of the earth and, apparently, she firmly believed that Kevin was alive. One of her other sons, Martin, was involved in a road accident not long after Lucy's murder. He was driving an Audi A4 when he lost control in Pighue Lane, Wavertree. His best friend, Joseph Mullin, was a passenger in the back seat. Both Mullin and Parle were flung from the car after it smashed into railings and a lamp post. Parle was severely injured and Mullin was killed.

While Martin was in hospital with his mum at his bedside, I'm told a Merseyside police detective turned up. Perhaps they were working on the theory that Kevin Parle might have come to visit his severely injured brother. By all accounts, Shirley and this officer had a bit of a heated conversation. As a result, Shirley firmly believes that the police have a shoot-to-kill policy with regard to Kevin and that, if they ever find him, her son will die.

The police service does not operate a shoot-to-kill policy. In the main, when the police shoot, they do so to stop people – to prevent the actions of those who pose a threat or to stop them from doing what they're doing. That is why they predominantly aim for the chest and abdomen area, for that is how you are most likely to stop someone. I should point out that a terrorist suspect who is believed to be wearing a suicide bomb vest will, if possible, be shot in the head, for reasons that should be obvious. Shirley, to this day, remains convinced that Kevin will be assassinated by the police. This thought was described to me as being her number one fear. Shirley wants her son home as long as he gets a fair trial. She would accept the consequences of any such trial, but back home, in the UK, is where she wants him. I was told that if such an offer was made, she would grab it with both hands.

This particular source also knew a fair bit about other criminality that Kevin was alleged to have been involved in. They said, 'The jobs he was up to would require a lot of planning and covert reconnaissance. He's got money stashed away – tens of thousands of pounds dotted around here and there – well, he did have, at the time the murders were committed.'

If a six-foot six-inch, broadly built man is capable of carrying out covert reconnaissance, then he's clearly no fool and this meeting served as another reminder for me of the calibre of wanted man that I was up against. This source reiterated what we'd discovered already; that Kevin Parle was a Liverpool supporter – a red.

I have quite a chequered history with Liverpool Football Club. It stretches back as far as the 1975/76 season, when my beloved Queens Park Rangers were top of the League with just a few days of the season left to go. Unfortunately, Liverpool had a game in hand against Wolverhampton Wanderers which they won and so they pipped us to the League title by the skinniest of margins – one point. I listened to that last game of the season on the radio. I was a teenager and devastated that we didn't win the League. It was probably our one and only chance of doing that. After the game, a mighty fine Liverpool player called John Toshack was asked, 'A word for Queens Park Rangers, who have played such wonderful football and pushed you all the way to the finish line?'

Toshack's reply was words to the effect of, 'We won. They didn't. Tough.' Just writing these words reminds me of how painful they were to hear all those years ago. I vowed that night that, if I ever saw John Toshack in the flesh, I would do unspeakable things to him. That was nonsense – he was a towering, muscular footballer and I was a skinny teen. Even so, ever since then I've taken great joy whenever any team managed by Toshack has lost. Irrational, juvenile, I know, but that's what football does to some of us. I had a smattering of revenge in 1986 when I had the huge pleasure of being at Anfield for the second leg of the League Cup semi-final. The game ended 2-2 with Liverpool players generously scoring two own goals for QPR and we went through to the final on an aggregate score of 3-2. Standing on the terraces at Anfield, singing to the koppites as they filed out dejectedly, 'We're going to Wembley, we're going to Wembley, you're not, you're not!' was a truly wonderful thing.

But, as per usual, when you support a football club like mine, the joy is so often short-lived. Don't ask me what happened in the final. A year or so later, on 18 March 1987, I was back at Anfield for a mid-week League game that Rangers duly lost 2-1. I travelled up on the supporters' coach and, when we returned after the game, we found that the windows had been bricked by Liverpool fans. They'd won but they still felt the compulsion to damage the opposition's transport. I, and my fellow QPR supporters, travelled all the way from Liverpool to London with a howling gale blowing through the gap where there used to be windows. The coach driver tried to cover the gap with black plastic bags and sticky tape but the minute we went above 20mph that all disappeared. Courtesy of Liverpool fans, we shivered and we froze all the way back to London. As a result, I've never had much of a love for Liverpool FC and its fans, but I realised I was going to have to park a lot of those feelings because I would be spending an awful lot of time in Liverpool over the course of the next few months.

The burner phone rang. A man told me that Kevin Parle had been seen in Liverpool within the last two years. I asked him how he knew this, and he told me his friend had seen Parle in a red Audi, stationary at a set of traffic lights. The eyewitness had apparently gone to school with Parle, knew him well and was absolutely certain that he recognised him. I was aware I was getting this information second-hand but, if it was true, then it was astonishing. I was extremely keen to learn more. I tasked the source to go back to his friend and ask some more questions. I wanted flesh on the bones. Could it really be that Parle had returned to his home city? It's a well-known fact that the lure of home is often irresistible for some fugitives, but would Parle have taken the risk of coming back and being spotted – just, in fact, as I was being told he had been – out and about on the streets? The source said he would get back to me.

Among the other people calling my burner phone was a former Merseyside detective who was now retired and living in the sunshine. All was well with life except for one thing; his retirement was blighted by the fact that Kevin Parle remained at large. This detective had worked on over a hundred murders in Liverpool, yet the thing that kept him awake at night was the fact that Kevin Parle 'took the piss out of us'. He was yet another who told me how intelligent Parle was – 'very, very clever'. At the end of our conversation where, in his words, 'We had spoken as one detective to another,' he wished me all the best, and reiterated that he would only truly be happy with life once Parle is 'banged away'.

Mark and I travelled home from Liverpool on the Thursday, a mere four days after my press conference – and what a trip it had been. Five sightings of Parle had been reported by various people. The source who had told me about Parle and the red Audi got back in touch. He said Parle had been visiting a cemetery somewhere in Liverpool. He didn't know any more – whether Parle was looking for a relative or a friend, paying respects or acting out of a sense of guilt (although I suspected the latter was highly unlikely) – but it gave us a bit more work to follow up on.

I had quite a bit of information on a reported sighting of Parle in Portugal, some five years earlier, when he had apparently been in the company of a woman in her thirties with dark hair. The person with this information said Parle had been exercising every day and didn't engage in conversation with anybody. This person was utterly convinced of the accuracy of their sighting.

Mark and I bought a bottle of wine and some snacks to enjoy on the train home, and reflected on the fact that just a few days earlier when we had gone into a pub everyone had said, 'Kevin who? Never heard of him' and, in the space of just a few days, that had changed. Now when we asked people about Parle, they were saying, 'Oh, yes, we read about him in the *Echo*,' or, 'We saw you on the BBC,' or, 'We know who he is. He really needs to be caught.' This was so pleasing because it was a central part of what I was trying to achieve – making Kevin Parle a well-known fugitive.

The trolls were still having a go. Twitter accounts without followers – in other words, recently set up for the sole purpose of trolling me – were sending the usual nonsense. It was a price worth paying for the progress that we were making. Mark had recorded quite a bit of stuff for the podcast pilot episode he was putting together so, all in all, time and money well spent. However, my hunt for Kevin Parle was now leaving me out of pocket. I needed to find some other paid work.

I'm a frequent contributor to a number of radio stations where I comment on crime and policing, and occasionally other subjects as diverse as parenting. I carry the title of the 'Radio 2 policeman' on the *Jeremy Vine* show, a programme that I've had the great pleasure of being a small part of for many years. I should point out that my role there does not come with a warrant card or any powers of arrest! I've also made countless contributions to talkRADIO. Generally speaking, they don't pay for an interview if it's done down the phone from home, and that's fine, I can live with that. The pay-off comes when I have something to promote, like a book, because then they let me on the radio and give me plenty of airtime to talk about it. It is an unofficial arrangement that I'm happy with.

talkRADIO asked, 'We'd like you to talk for ten minutes on our show at 1 a.m. about your hunt for Parle.' I negotiated an hour to talk about Parle at length. I wanted to discuss the crimes he was wanted for as well as my hunt. I didn't know how big the audience was at that time of night but, regardless, I felt this was an opportunity not to be missed. At 12.15 a.m., while most of the nation slept, I jumped into my car and headed to central London. Presenter Paul Ross, older brother of Jonathan, and I had met a number of times over the years. Paul was really interested in what I had to say and gave me a free rein. I was envious of him. In my wildest dreams I would be a night-time radio presenter, but I fear my chances of ever landing a job like that may have passed me by.

I didn't hold back. Some listeners rang in with good questions and the hour flew by. Just after 2 a.m., I was in the car and driving home. I loved the deserted streets of London. I passed through a couple of the areas where I had worked as a cop all those years ago. Memories flooded back. I relished night duty. For me, there is something truly magical about working while the nation sleeps and we had many fantastic successes, particularly against burglars trying to break into commercial premises in the small hours.

I smiled to myself as I recalled one operation during which we followed a team of very accomplished burglars from the Home Counties as they met up with one another, performed their anti-surveillance tactics (unsuccessfully, as I was able to observe first-hand), swapped vehicles and drove into central London to start breaking into a high-end jeweller. I had sight of the team from the end of an alleyway where I was hidden in the shadows. I was the 'eyeball', in old-school surveillance terms. The crooks simply never saw me as they set about disabling the alarm and drilling into the front door. Through my covert radio I told my colleagues to move closer. In my earpiece I could hear my team taking up position. We let the burglars get into the jewellers, waiting a few minutes before we pounced. The villains were absolutely bang to rights with their tools, their bags of swag and their crestfallen faces. They knew what was now inevitable: a considerable spell inside.

After I got home following the interview, I checked my phone and was delighted to see an email from a man who has become very important to me in my hunt for Parle, who I will call Kyle. I was grateful that many open-source intelligence operatives, ethical hackers and others had offered to help, it had become clear at this early stage of the hunt that I needed one person to do the bulk of this work. A large number of people all doing a little bit of research work here and there was going to be problematic. There might be unnecessary duplication, more people might get to know what I knew, and there was the risk of an inadvertent leak of information to Parle or his associates. Collating the disparate evidence would be more time-consuming.

Kyle knew I didn't have any money to pay him. Despite the fact that he had family commitments and that he also has to earn a living, he volunteered to be my main man. He went on to be, quite simply, brilliant. When Parle is captured Kyle knows that a fully paid trip to London, including travel, hotel, food and beer awaits him. He is very much looking forward to that. That email detailed the results of research so far and there would be much more to come.

Not long after I'd returned home from Liverpool, one of my two teenage boys explained that he was worried about what I was doing. The family was at the dinner table when he became upset and, very emotionally, revealed his fear that criminals might seek to do me or them some harm. He said he wanted to change his name and that he was taking his social media profiles down. I tried to reassure him, as did my wife, but some things are unavoidable. She said, 'Dad has a really unusual name. There's not much we can do about that. If they want to find him and do him some harm, then they will. But you're just going to have to trust your dad.'

I must admit I thought to myself, what the fuck have I started here? Had I thought this out properly? I was only a week or so into the hunt and now one of my kids was very worried. Later on that night I tried to reassure him. I sat on the edge of his bed and told him a bit about my life as an undercover cop, how I'd lived under witness protection and survived, and how I felt that Parle and his cronies were probably more concerned about me and what I was going to discover than I was about them. I explained, perhaps clumsily, that the worst thing that could happen was that I would get a bullet in my head. But I've lived for nearly sixty years, I've had a very good life. I don't want to die, but if it happens, so be it. And if that did happen, there'd be an enormous investigation launched and it would direct an awful lot of unwanted attention towards Parle and his associates: that would be a daft thing for them to bring down on themselves. I'm not entirely convinced that he was consoled by what I had to say but he got the message, I was not going to stop.

The following week I went on Sky News and had a twenty-five-minute chat with presenter Kay Burley. I was able to hold up my Kevin Parle flyers to the cameras and reach out to yet another audience. I know that Kay is a 'Marmite' figure. Well, I like her – I like her a lot. In 2019 I climbed Scafell Pike with her and a few others in aid of charity. She looked after me wonderfully and ensured that I safely got to the top and back down again. That night we had a thoroughly enjoyable evening sharing a few glasses of wine and some food. I shall firmly remain a fan of the wonderful Kay Burley. A couple of days later I was on Jeremy Vine's Channel 5 television show, once again talking about Kevin Parle. All this publicity was having an effect because my burner phone kept on ringing as people were getting in touch. The majority of these people were very well-intentioned and this public interest was terrific.

9

LIVERPOOL TWO

It was less than three weeks since we'd returned from our first trip to Liverpool and Mark and I were on our way back.

This time we'd hired a car and on the way north we stopped off at Professor David Wilson's house. David is the emeritus professor of criminology at Birmingham City University and an absolute world leader in his field. He gave us an interview for the podcast and we asked him to give his opinion on Parle, based on what we'd discovered about him thus far. It was still relatively early days and the information I could give David was fairly limited. He was to give us a far more insightful description of Parle a few months later, when he had a whole heap of testimonies to rely upon. After an enjoyable couple of hours, Mark and I continued on our way to Liverpool.

My agent rang. My website had been hacked and the tech guy was going to move it onto a more secure server. I saw this development as a positive thing, just like the trolling. If people were going to the bother of hacking my website and trolling me, it begged the question, why? Because Parle was alive and these were efforts to intimidate me, that was why.

In the run-up to this trip I had been in touch with an English-language newspaper published in Spain. Their target audience is made up of 800,000 or so British expats. I wanted to contact the journalist who reported in 2006 that Kevin Parle, while on the run, had been spotted in a holiday park in Torrevieja on the Costa Blanca, and that a member of staff at the park had described Parle as a 'gentle giant'. Perhaps I could find the person who gave that quote. They'd reprinted a large part of that original article a few years later when Merseyside police made another public appeal for information about Parle. Despite the article being years earlier, sometimes you just don't know what you might discover about someone when you delve a long way back into their past. Past behaviour is often an indicator of the future. Unfortunately, the journalist had moved on and his employers had no way of contacting him, but the paper was interested in my hunt for Parle. I gave them an interview. I was grateful for the column inches when the article was duly published a few days later along with my contact details.

As Mark and I were driving to Liverpool my phone burner rang. It was a woman who lived and worked in Spain. She had seen the article about Parle and told me that, a few days after reading it, she had been in a bar in Dénia, in the north of the Costa Blanca. She went on to explain that she had overheard a group of people discussing Parle and was convinced that they actually knew him. Unfortunately, she hadn't heard the precise details of their conversation, but she was sure that she had heard a man say, 'We know people that can make people disappear.' I was pleased and frustrated in equal measure. Pleased that this lady had rung me, but frustrated that her recollection was so light on detail.

We were back in the budget hotel in Liverpool. Mark and I set about the business of finding stuff out. I was contacted again by the former Merseyside detective and, among a few useful snippets, he shared a chat-up line that Parle apparently brazenly delivered to young women he met out in public: 'We should do breakfast some time.' Maybe it's my age, but I find that line rather nauseating. However, I was going to get it to the public, to see if it prompted anyone's memory or provoked Parle or his associates.

On 23 May 2019 we had arranged to meet the DCI from Merseyside police. I recorded a quick interview for BBC Radio Merseyside. It wasn't live because Mark and I had deliberately decided to travel under the radar this time. No publicity, no social media postings, just me and Mark making our way quietly around the city, in large part because we'd arranged to meet the police. We didn't want anybody to know that; I had to remain vigilant to the fact that some people might want to put us under surveillance. After the radio interview Mark and I drove for about twenty-five minutes to an extremely secure, brand-new police facility. It was a stunning building; modern, but I thought it was beautiful.

We were stopped at the gate and questioned by security, showed our ID and headed to the visitors' car park. We were let through turnstiles similar to those you might find at a football ground, and we made our way over to reception where once again we introduced ourselves. We were told to take a seat and we waited for a few minutes. And we waited … and we waited a little bit longer. The DCI and his DI eventually came down, greeted us warmly with handshakes, warmly but professionally, and then took us on a short tour of the building. They were clearly very proud of it, rightfully so – it had cost over fifty million pounds. They explained how they now had all their investigative specialisms under one roof which was a great help. In a very functional meeting room, we exchanged pleasantries and small talk while we waited for coffees to arrive and then the DCI produced his notebook and pen and the meeting began.

We explained that Mark was making the podcast pilot episode, and how we hoped that the series would get commissioned. We told them what we hoped the podcast might achieve in terms of public awareness and the potential for help in finding Parle. Fairly early in the proceedings I reiterated the fact that I had no intention of embarrassing Merseyside police. The DI instantly leant forward and firmly said, 'We will not be embarrassed.'

The DCI explained that everybody was now talking about Parle, including uniform cops who were asking him what the detectives were doing about finding him. I was thrilled to hear this. If Parle was now the talk of the police service, that could only be a good thing. The officers explained that they felt my research might uncover evidence or information about other serious crimes and I said it might do, but that I had deliberately focused solely on Kevin Parle. I wasn't interested in discovering who was supplying drugs and guns or, indeed, committing any other form of crime. I told the detectives that my deliberately narrow parameters would ensure that the only information I would get for them would be in relation to the hunt for Parle.

Even though we'd previously discussed the reward on the phone, I felt that it was so important that I asked the DCI to confirm that the twenty thousand pounds for Parle's arrest and conviction still stood. He said it did but went on to reiterate that the reward was subject to Parle being convicted of both crimes. I told him again that I thought that condition was very unfair, and I unapologetically hypothesised; I said to him, 'Say, for example, a very well-meaning member of the public provides the information that leads to Parle's arrest and he subsequently stands trial for both murders. It is widely known that Tony Downes and Kirk Bradley were acquitted of Lucy's murder so if the same was to happen to Parle, that would be rather unfair on the person who had provided the information, particularly if Parle was convicted of Liam's murder.'

The DCI replied, 'We would have to adopt a pragmatic view in those circumstances.' I asked him if the reward would be paid if somebody gave me information that led to me finding Parle dead. Again, he said they would have to 'take a view'. I was a bit concerned about how this 'pragmatic view' might be manifested, but decided that if it did come about, it would mean that Parle had been caught in one way or another and that would be a nice problem to have at some point in the future.

I told the DCI that I wasn't interested in claiming the reward for myself under any circumstances, but if somebody were to use me as a conduit to pass the information through to the police, then I was happy to act as a middle-man in order to protect the identity of my source. By the looks on their faces I don't think the detectives were very thrilled at the prospect. During my former career with the police, I wrote many, many reward reports, applying for informant cash, and the template for those letters was seared in my brain. And it was only right that someone was able to choose me to protect their identity. I think the police were horrified at the prospect of having to give me so much money on the promise that I would hand it on to another person. And in all probability that reward scenario was not going to come about, but in case it did I wanted to lay down some ground rules.

The DCI said I was now a registered confidential source – an informant, in other words – although in the truest sense of the term, I wasn't. I was a conduit, a person through whom people could get information passed to the police without their identities being revealed. Thank goodness it's me taking this role and not anyone less experienced, I thought, thinking back to the way in which two more traditional informants – or grasses or snitches – that I had handled during my time at New Scotland Yard had both come to very sticky ends.

In April 1991, a man called David Norris was gunned down in a professional hit outside his house in Belvedere, south-east London. A motorbike pulled up as he got out of his car and he was shot a number of times by the pillion passenger. Norris fell to the ground, fatally wounded, and died in his partner's arms. He had been a prolific police informant who would have grassed up his granny if there had been a few quid in it for him. He had introduced me to gangs when I was working undercover and a number of the operations I was involved with against them had been successful. Norris also provided information to other squads that had led to countless villains being banged up and, at the time of his death, it was almost an open secret in the criminal circles of south London and beyond: he was a grass. He was addicted to it. He loved the thrill, he loved the buzz and he particularly enjoyed the enormous sums of money that Scotland Yard paid for his information. Unlike some of my colleagues, I never got particularly close to him. I was always careful to ensure that he was at arm's length. Other detectives became very chummy – perhaps too close to him.

I last spoke to Norris just a matter of minutes before he was gunned down. He rang me from a pub where he was having a drink with yet another detective to whom he was no doubt passing information. I was on my way to meet him the following morning when I heard on the radio a man had been shot and killed in Belvedere. I knew immediately it had to be Norris. I was with a colleague – he had been expecting to collect a few quid from Norris over a betting coup that they'd pulled off that weekend – and he crumbled in front of my very eyes. I had to drive him back to my flat and give him a stiff brandy while he pulled himself together. A couple of people were later convicted of conspiracy but the man who rode the motorcycle and the man who pulled the trigger were never convicted.

Another informant, Peter McNeil, provided us with some astonishing information into a mafia-run cocaine smuggling operation. I didn't work as closely with him as I had done with Norris, but we'd met on a number of occasions and, quite frankly, I didn't warm to the man. He had a superior and supercilious air and looked down his nose at a lowly detective like me. He was forty years old and living under the name of James Lawson in Hampshire when, in February 1998, he was shot dead in his home. McNeil's information had directly led to us seizing what was then the biggest amount of cocaine ever found in the UK and some people have long memories – particularly the mafia.

One of the men arrested for that plot, David Medin, was an American gangster who found himself staring down the barrel of a hefty jail sentence. He decided to turn supergrass and give evidence against the man he claimed as his co-plotter. That all turned out to be an utter waste of time and money – the man later had his conviction quashed at the court of appeal.

Now I was myself a registered police source for Merseyside police and the upside for me personally was they would now have a duty of care. That wasn't to say that they were going to tuck me in at night and guard my front door 24/7 but if they received intelligence that suggested I was going to come to harm, they would be duty-bound to tell me. If the information they received was not sufficient to make arrests, charge people and put them in front of a court, then they would have to issue me with an Osman warning. These are given from time to time to criminals or informants whose lives are under threat so that they can alter their lives accordingly. I'm delighted to report that as of the time of writing I have not had one – at least, not yet.

I asked the detectives what they thought about the rumours that Kevin Parle was dead. The DCI replied, 'I am keeping an open mind on that.'

Our meeting drew to a close, and it had been overwhelmingly cordial. Without question, the police were the epitome of twenty-first-century professional detectives, and our hour together passed very quickly. The DCI looked me in the eye and said, 'Best of luck.' We were escorted to the front door and Mark and I walked back to the car park in absolute silence. We were both waiting to get in our car before telling each other what we were thinking.

We negotiated the turnstiles, jumped in the car, slammed the doors shut, looked at each other and I said, 'He's alive.' Mark agreed wholeheartedly. That was the dominant thought we had both taken away from that meeting, even though the police hadn't even hinted that they believed Parle was still alive. It would now be down to me to prove that that was indeed the case.

We drove away and I introduced Mark to a phrase that old-sweat detectives like me used to say back in the day. It was how we'd describe a detective or uniformed officer who we knew we really wouldn't want to come up against if we were criminals ourselves – 'I wouldn't want to be nicked by him, or her.' I thought this saying applied to the DCI because of the professional way in which he had presented himself and the authority he exuded. He gave the impression of being a very competent operator. He also had a poker face which rarely, if ever, gave a flicker of emotion or insight into what he was thinking. I'm sure the likelihood of me ever playing poker with him would never arise, but it if did, I think he would relieve me of all my dosh.

We spent the rest of our time in Liverpool knocking on doors, engaging with those who would give us the time of day and putting flyers and business cards through people's letterboxes. There were a considerable number of people to visit who were of interest to my hunt, either because they were known to have been previously associated with Parle, or because I had been told they were currently or recently connected to him in one way or another.

We sometimes got information from the least promising sources. I had a phone conversation with someone who had first contacted my agent in the middle of the night. When I spoke to this person over the following day, he demanded seven thousand pounds to tell me what he knew. That was never going to happen – not only did I not have seven grand to give him but in any case I'm certainly not in the business of giving people huge amounts of money before they tell me what they know. This tail was not going to wag the dog. Bit by bit, this source began to let things slip. I rang him again and this time he'd reduced his demand by half. Nice try but, once again, he was whistling in the wind. That conversation was quite a short one. The following day he rang me and told me everything that he knew in return for absolutely no cash. He gave me the name of a notorious Liverpool criminal who had been arrested abroad towards the end of 2015. He suggested that I research this person, his contacts and his associates, both in the criminal and business worlds because he was convinced this man was connected to Parle.

Around the time that Mark and I were driving from one side of the city to the other and from the north to the south, handing out hundreds of flyers, and visiting numerous addresses, Liverpool Football Club had reached the final of the Champions League. They had staged a remarkable comeback against Barcelona in the second leg of the semi-final, which they won 4-0. We passed thousands of houses covered in flags, banners, and scarves, draped from windows and roofs. It was astonishing to see such a large proportion of the city united behind their football club. Pop-up market-type stalls appeared in pub car parks and on driveways, all selling Liverpool memorabilia, the majority of which appeared to be T-shirts.

At one point we stopped at a less than glamorous pub that had a stall out front. We grabbed Diet Cokes and on the way out I had a look at the merchandise. I had in mind a friend of my younger son. This mate of his is a Liverpool follower – I call him a 'follower' because he's not a supporter. He's never been to Anfield, never watched them play live and while I know he's a kid he's what I still describe as a 'plastic fan'. I pull his leg about it all the time in a very warm and affectionate way, because I adore this young fella. He tells me that the reason he supports Liverpool is because his dad did. Well, his dad was a Londoner and grew up in the heyday of Liverpool's successes and was clearly just a glory-seeker, because he's never been to Anfield either. Nevertheless, I handed over my tenner for a T-shirt – a bit steep, I thought; it seemed clear this T-shirt would only survive about two washes in the machine – and handed flyers to the likely lad working on the stall and his partner, who was sitting at a table with her young kids.

The man glanced at the appeal for information and said, 'I can't help you because I'm on the other side.'

His phrase irritated me. I said, 'Let's just get this straight; you are on a "side" that thinks the shooting of a sixteen-year-old boy and a twenty-two-year-old mother of three young children is OK. Have I got that right?'

He looked a bit uncomfortable and said, 'Well, I'm just telling you that I'm on the other side, so I can't speak to you.'

I wasn't going to let this go. 'But your side thinks those kinds of murders are OK, do they?' He didn't answer me. 'Just have a think about what you've said. Look at your partner – she's probably about the same age that Lucy was when she was murdered. Would you still be on the other side if somebody gunned her down?' We left on pretty reasonable terms, but I quite simply hadn't been able to allow him to get away with saying what he had, without me giving him a piece of my mind. His partner seemed very interested in what I was doing because she asked me for a few more flyers and I happily obliged. The more that get out there, the better: I work on the ratio of about one response from every hundred flyers. Historically, that's how it's generally happened. We got in the car and kept going.

I often find that barbers hear a lot of useful local information. Mark and I decided to take the plunge and have a haircut in Norris Green, an area that had attracted considerable notoriety over the years. True to form the barbers were both chatty and knowledgeable about the

'Nogga', as the area is sometimes called. They were keen to tell us about the strong sense of community that prevailed. A few lads and lasses were hanging about outside, and a couple of imaginatively dressed young fellas, who I would not have wanted to have a row with, kept an eye on me as I explained why I was in Liverpool.

There was a lovely moment when the barber cutting my hair hurriedly stopped what he was doing and ran out of the front door. He shouted at a kid who had just dropped a plastic drinks bottle on the pavement, 'You gonna leave that there?' The youngster needed no more persuasion to pick the bottle up and put it in the bin.

My haircut was finished before Mark's, so I stepped outside for a fag. Even though I was surrounded by lively looking young people, one of who was toking on a joint the size of a baby's arm, I felt completely at ease, and safe. A couple of the lads threw a glance and a nod in my direction. I replied with slight bow of the head, as if to convey to them that I accepted that I was very much on their turf.

We went to speak with a florist whose business was on the same parade of shops as the barber. He had run his business in Norris Green for forty-nine years. He was a lovely man. He had been a victim of crime on a couple of occasions over the years, but his towering local status had meant that justice of some description had usually been meted out to those responsible. He took great pride in modestly telling us about how he'd often helped out those experiencing hard times. He recalled how a grown man had returned to his shop many, many years after committing a minor crime as a child, for which the florist had given him a thoughtful and suitable tongue-lashing, laced with life advice, which had prompted the miscreant teenager to turn his life around. Tears welled in his eyes as his recounted this tale. You know the drill by now – we left him with a pile of flyers.

We visited the part of the city where Parle had lived as a kid. It was a very pleasant neighbourhood, a mixture of detached and semi-detached houses, many of which had been extended. A lot of time and attention had clearly been affectionately lavished upon the majority of these homes, typified by well-tended gardens and careful paintwork. We spoke to a few young families who had moved into the area long after the Parle family had moved on.

One man who had lived in the street for decades said the three Parle brothers had all been 'big lads, but they kept themselves to themselves'. The street appeared to be a nice one on which to raise your kids. It stood in stark contrast to some of the other parts of the city we had visited in our attempts to connect with people who knew Parle as an adult.

Another Diet Coke was needed on this humid and sunny day. We popped into a local pub. The landlady greeted us warmly and knew exactly who I was. Even so, she didn't escape a flyer. As I returned our empty glasses to the bar and thanked her, she fired me a wink, a smile and a 'Good luck.' This lady was clearly another Liverpudlian on the side of righteousness.

We drove to the home of Valerie Bradley. Crime has impacted on this lady in an enormous way. In 2011 her forty-nine-year-old son, Trevor Bradley, was jailed for his part in a large-scale cannabis plot. In 2012, her grandson, Kirk Bradley, son of Trevor, who'd been acquitted of Lucy's murder a few years earlier, was sentenced to life imprisonment with a minimum term of twenty-two years, for a campaign of fear and intimidation that involved guns and grenades. Anthony 'Fat Tony' Downes received the same sentence for the same offences. You will remember that Downes had also been acquitted of Lucy's murder, alongside Bradley. In 2013, Valerie's grandson Karl Bradley, another one of Trevor's sons, and Kirk's brother, was shot dead. After enduring that bellyful of upset, in November 2016 a motorcycle pulled up outside Valerie's house and the pillion passenger fired a number of gunshots at the front door. One of these bullets hit Valerie and shattered her leg.

I thought Valerie might be an interesting person to talk to. Mark parked the car in a street around the corner and we approached the modest and tidy-looking terraced house on foot. Valerie was sat in a chair in the front garden, her head tilted slightly back. She appeared to be enjoying the sunshine. A muscular man in his forties sat at a table just a few feet away. A similarly aged woman was chatting to Valerie. A handsome dog lolloped around.

We stood outside the front gate and I introduced us both. The man took hold of the dog, put it into the house and we were invited to enter the front garden. One of the first things I did was to ask Valerie about her leg. She explained that she was still having difficulty walking properly, and that it was painful at times. I sympathised with her. I made it perfectly clear that I was only interested in finding Parle, and that I was not investigating any wider criminality. I told all three of them that I would like to speak to Kirk and that I would happily visit him in prison. Valerie promised that she would speak to Kirk's mother, who apparently visited him regularly in prison and Valerie said she would pass on my flyer and business card to her.

We had a short natter about the weather and some other inconsequential stuff, before we wished everybody well, exchanged handshakes, and left. The man did not utter one word throughout, while Valerie was polite, engaging and rather lovely.

Once Mark and I got back in the car, we had a discussion about how wise it was for me to be giving out not only my burner phone number, but my personal phone details to a member of the Bradley family. I didn't have a problem with it. This hunt for Parle was about building bridges, gaining people's trust and, in all likelihood, I would need to gain the trust of people involved in, or on the margins of, very serious crime. I'm not suggesting for a moment that Valerie has been involved in crime, but some of her family members clearly are or have been. In the event, I never heard a word from any member of the Bradley family. It was a shame really because I would quite happily have spent more time in Valerie's company. Valerie, if you're reading this, you have my number, both of them in fact. And my email address.

It took us twelve minutes to cover the five-mile drive to Pennard Avenue, the scene of the 1993 fatal car accident. It was here that four-year-old Kevin Downes was hit and killed by the stolen car driven by teenager Andrew Ellis, alongside passenger Gary Campbell. Mark and I were both in a sombre mood as we shoved flyers through letterboxes. The death of any child is always a tragedy. An utterly unnecessary death like Kevin's must leave enduring pain. We met a man who told us that he lived in Pennard Avenue at the time of the crash. He said that he knew Tony Downes and that he'd get a message to him in prison. I spoke to another man who, all these years later, was still enraged at the fact that the teenage driver of the stolen car that killed Kevin Downes, Andrew Ellis, was only locked up for twelve months, the maximum sentence that could be handed down at the time. The law was changed shortly afterwards, and the maximum possible sentence was revised upwards to ten years. It all came too late for those who wanted to see Andrew Ellis serve longer in custody.

The opportunity to do some media interviews arose and, as it was by now no longer a secret that I was in town, I was more than happy to do them. I gave a recorded interview to Radio City in their studios at the top of the 138-metre tall Radio City Tower, smack-bang in the centre of town. The views from the top of the tower are absolutely wonderful – do make sure a trip is on your to-do list the next time you are in Liverpool. I cannot recommend it enough.

It was getting late by the time we got back to the hotel bar. Mark got a bottle of white wine, and I got a bottle of red. It was a balmy evening and we sat at my favourite spot at the back, overlooking the docks. We ruminated over the couple of days we'd had. Inevitably, our conversation drifted to Parle and where he might be. I was now becoming concerned that the media attention I was getting might drive him further underground, take him even further away from the radar and make him impossible to find, especially if the police were not proactively looking for him.

These nagging self-doubts about how I was conducting my hunt plagued me frequently then – and still do. I tried to console myself by imagining out loud to Mark that Parle's cronies were saying to him, 'Do what you've done for the past fourteen years, Kev. Don't rise to any of this. Sit tight and let it all blow over. This stupid, old has-been will write his rubbish book and then move onto something else.' I was also far from convinced that the BBC was going to commission the podcast. Around 11 p.m., with the bravery that came from having a couple of glasses of red inside me, I told Mark this. I pride myself on being an optimist, but I've been a part of many development projects – be they TV dramas, documentaries or ideas for radio – that have never ended up getting a green light. Mark told me to park my negativity elsewhere because, following our two trips to Liverpool, he felt he was gathering some very good audio. My pessimism would later rear its ugly head on our next trip, again after a couple of glasses of red and again, by mere chance, at 11 p.m. After this, 11 p.m. became known to Mark and I as 'It-will-never-get-commissioned o'clock.'

The following morning we had some meetings lined up, after first walking to Albert Dock to get some breakfast. On the way Mark told me that he was yearning for smashed avocado. I'd never had it before. We sat down in a rather rustic-looking, but not fancy, dockside café, I ordered the same as him, smashed avocado on toast. I nearly gagged when it arrived: it looked like a plate of dog vomit. I smothered it in pepper and gave it a go. I was very pleasantly surprised. I'm now a convert.

We ended up driving back to London on what was a Friday afternoon and, as a result, we had to suffer an enormous amount of traffic. The only upside of this was it gave us a lot of time to strategise and plot the way forward. After many hours of driving, Mark kindly dropped me off at my local cricket club so I could enjoy a pint and a burger. It meant that he got home a lot later than I did, but I was to repay the favour some months later.

10

MY FIRST CHOICE

I planned to spend the day after our return from Liverpool relaxing and watching my youngest son play cricket. Fat chance of that.

In the morning, I was contacted by two former detectives who I'd worked with, one of whom had seen the article in the Spanish newspaper and was keen to tell me that he had a property on the Costa Blanca. I never really got on with him when we worked together because he wasn't what I would have called a first-division tec. He always seemed more interested in playing hard without doing the working hard bit. And he had a bit too much money for my liking, bearing in mind that we were of the same rank, lowly detective constables. I wasn't comfortable with his approach and I didn't follow it up.

The other former detective was, by contrast, an absolutely top guy who used to be on the police boxing team with me, and was a far better fighter than I was. I trusted him implicitly and I didn't have any problem telling him a fair bit about what I knew, if not everything, for obvious reasons. He suggested some contacts that he thought I should reach out to and the rest of the day was swallowed up doing that.

The next day was Sunday 26 May, 2019, which was Kevin Parle's thirty-ninth birthday. The thought of him having a party, enjoying himself, maybe having a drink, a girlfriend draped on his arm sickened me, as I'm sure it would many others. I was really hoping that he wouldn't be at liberty to enjoy his fortieth.

The next week the *Sun* got in touch with me. They hadn't come to the press conference but, because of the publicity I was getting elsewhere, it appeared they were suddenly interested in Kevin Parle. The *Sun* was roundly hated and boycotted on Merseyside because of the scandalous headlines it printed after the Hillsborough disaster of April 1989 that claimed the lives of ninety-six Liverpool supporters at the FA Cup semi-final against Nottingham Forest.

I remember the day of Hillsborough vividly. I was watching QPR play out a turgid 0-0 draw against Middlesbrough. My mate sitting next to me was listening to a portable radio and he told me the news that someone had died at Hillsborough, and then he passed on the details of another death, and then another, as the tragedy unfolded. I'd been going to football stadiums since I was a kid. There are not many grounds in England that I haven't been to. I've been subjected to good and bad football policing. I policed a few games myself when I was in uniform. As me and my mate lost interest in the QPR game and started discussing the events at Hillsborough I told him, 'This is down to the police. The crowd is their responsibility.'

It was great testimony to the determination and fortitude of Hillsborough campaigners that the unnecessary and entirely avoidable loss of life was not buried in the annals of history like so much of the establishment wanted it to be. That tragic story still has many twists and turns to come. I needed to put my relationship with the people of Liverpool in front of the needs of the *Sun*. I steered the journalist in another direction. If they wanted to find out any information about Parle they could do it themselves. I didn't need them to be my ally.

In the early hours of 29 May, I was sitting in front of my laptop, a glass of whiskey in my hand, and I was pondering as my family slept. It was exactly a month since I had launched my hunt for Parle. I'd had various sightings reported, I'd met with the police, and all in all I felt it had been a productive month. I had become irritated at times, particularly when speaking to people who clearly knew more than they were letting on and when people who were most definitely at home refused to answer the door. I wondered what the attitude of some of these people would be if their sixteen-year-old son or twenty-two-year-old daughter had been killed. Would they want someone like me to be out there trying to find the person wanted for such a crime, some fifteen years later? I'm pretty sure they would. As far as I was concerned there was no middle ground if you know something that might help me, but you say to yourself, 'I don't want to get involved.' If that is the case, then you're putting yourself firmly on the side of Kevin Parle. End of. We all make mistakes, and we all have the right to change our minds, of course we do. Anybody who is having a change of mind while reading this is very welcome to contact me, I'd be delighted and utterly forgiving to hear from you.

I also appreciate that some people might be very frightened about telling me what they know. Criminals who use firearms are scary people. But remaining silent only empowers them. It increases the chances of these pathetic people picking up a gun once again. And on that occasion, they may use it on you or someone close to you, or some other entirely innocent member of the public. What kind of world do we want to live in? Who do we want to govern our streets and our way of life? Our police may not be perfect, but I'd rather a cop with a gun than a crook.

I've often heard cynical cops say, 'The public gets the police they deserve.' I detest that expression with a passion. The public should get the very best possible police service imaginable. I appreciate that we don't live in the ideal world, but the cops should always put service before self and the public before promotion.

I decided to check the Interpol and Europol websites for Parle. To my horror, he did not feature on either. These organisations are front and centre of so much worldwide cooperation between police forces and their efforts to track wanted fugitives: his face should most certainly have featured heavily on both. I pointed this out in an email to the DCI. Yet, to this day, Parle is not on either website. It makes me wonder exactly how committed the police are to catching him.

I pored over the Merseyside police website as well. There was not a word about Kevin Parle. There still isn't as I write this today, despite me pointing that out to the DCI. The only law enforcement website to mention Parle is the National Crime Agency and there at least he features on their most-wanted list. On more than one occasion I sat in the car, mulling over things with Mark and saying, 'Are we the only people on planet Earth that want him caught?' It felt like that sometimes.

Kevin Parle had not been my first choice of quarry. When I decided to hunt a real fugitive, I made my mind up to go after a man called Shane O'Brien. That particular piece of garbage killed a wonderful young man called Josh Hanson, in a bar in Eastcote, north-west London in the early hours of Sunday 11 October, 2015.

Josh and some friends had merely gone for a night out, to have a few drinks and a bit of fun and Josh was only twenty-one. He was a hugely popular lad who worked hard, put family first, and had a wide circle of friends who adored him. O'Brien, by stark contrast, was a career criminal, a man of violence with convictions for carrying weapons. Essentially, he was an oxygen thief. In an utterly unprovoked and unjustifiable act of savage brutality, he slashed Josh with a Stanley knife, before, in the finest tradition of pathetic cowardice, going on the run. Shamefully, there were a number of people willing to help O'Brien. He was flown out of the UK on a private plane from Biggin Hill airport in Kent and then vanished.

Tracey Hanson, Josh's mum, was and is a truly remarkable woman. I have never met a more inspirational person in my life. It is with the greatest of pride that I tell you she is my friend. The grief and shock of losing her beautiful son spurred Tracey on to conduct a worldwide campaign to raise awareness of O'Brien's status as a fugitive. She harvested the support of family, friends and, quite literally, tens of thousands of people. Wanted posters were stuck to lamp posts, windows, fences and more, around the world. Tracey's home became the nerve centre of her operation. She engaged with the media in a manner that would shame experienced campaigners. On one notable occasion she stood outside Victoria station, London, wearing a sandwich board with a picture of O'Brien's ugly mush. She handed flyers to commuters coming off their trains as Sky News filmed her. There was more, much more, but I hope you read all about that in her upcoming book.

O'Brien had been on the run for over three years when I decided I would go after him. I was given Tracey's phone number by a mutual acquaintance and we got on like a house on fire. Tracey was very pleased that I was going to help with her search. I explained my plans and tactics, and she was more than happy about the idea. I spent the next three weeks researching and planning a book, reading every word ever printed about O'Brien, and there was quite a bit. I studied what the police had done and noticed they had antagonised the O'Brien family by their presence at a family funeral. Nevertheless, as I explained to Tracey, I would ideally be reaching out to the O'Brien family in an effort to get them onside. Such a move might be unpalatable to her as a member of the victim's family; however, Tracey took the news in her stride and raised no objection. She appreciated that I might use tactics the police would or could not deploy, but I had also promised her that I would keep her feelings at the centre of everything I did. It was the very least I could do for this remarkable woman.

I'd already spread the word among friends and former colleagues about my new project. I had also contacted a lot of people who I hoped would be onside. Then one day my phone went into meltdown, O'Brien had been captured in Romania. I was absolutely delighted, especially for the redoubtable Tracey.

Having spent three and a half years on the run, O'Brien at last stood in the dock at the Old Bailey in October 2019. Tracey and I had kept in touch and I attended the trial whenever my other work commitments would allow. Just because O'Brien had been captured, that didn't mean that I was going to disappear from Tracey's life. She had placed her trust in me, and we had shared conversations in which she had bared her soul.

I met many of her wonderful family and friends who helped her through the ghastly ordeal that was the trial. It was made all the worse because O'Brien ran a shameful defence, claiming that he had acted in self-defence. This pathetic effort to wriggle off the hook was shown up for the pack of lies that it was. The court was told how O'Brien had inflicted a 37cm-long wound to Josh that began at his ear, crossed his throat – which was sliced open – and ran down through his chest. The jury saw through the disgraceful and hurtful lies and rightfully found O'Brien guilty of murder. I was in the packed public gallery of the court to see the judge sentence him to life imprisonment with a minimum of twenty-six years.

Tracey, her family and many of Josh's friends retired to a local bar once the case was finished. I joined them. They were a lovely bunch of people. I wasn't drinking because I had to drive one of my sons around later that evening. Emotions were mixed. There was certainly no cause for wild celebration because everyone still desperately missed Josh and his love, his humour and his smile. I was actually rather cross. O'Brien was then thirty-one years old, so if he did become eligible for release after he had served his twenty-six years, he would be younger than I am now when he next tastes freedom. That didn't seem right to me. I strongly felt he should have got longer, but the judge had to abide by fairly rigid sentencing guidelines. I made my considerable irritation at all of this known to Tracey. I wasn't sure if I was doing the right thing, and a large part of me was telling me just to shut up, but my anger boiled over. True to form, Tracey let me pour my heart out. She then told me exactly what she thought: 'The sentence is a joke. Life should mean life.' I couldn't agree more. Before I left the pub she asked me if I was OK. Me? What the hell did it matter how I was? I'd not just seen a man sentenced for murdering my beloved son but Tracey Hanson is one of those astonishing people who put the feelings of others above her own.

A few weeks later I paid a visit to Tracey's home along with a TV producer. By now Tracey was fully aware that I had shifted my attention to Parle and I picked her brains at length about her campaign to find O'Brien. The police have never publicly credited Tracey with finding him, but it is undeniable that her relentless work shrunk the world for O'Brien in a way that may well have led to his capture. Before we left, she looked me in the eye and gave me some sage advice about my own hunt. 'This is a campaign. Do not lose your focus. Do not run out of steam.'

Trust me, Tracey, I won't.

Tracey continues to do courageous and selfless work. She takes her story into schools and other institutions in an effort to prevent people from picking up weapons and killing one another. She campaigns to put right what she feels is so wrong about our criminal justice system and the way that victims and their families are treated. Please look her up online and follow her. Anyone with a soul will be uplifted and inspired by her.

11

LIVERPOOL THREE

The 2019 Champions League Final was looming on 1 June. It was going to be played in Madrid, Spain, where Liverpool would face Spurs. The English-language Spanish newspaper that I had talked to were particularly interested in this fixture, as they speculated Parle might go to the game. I spoke to one of their journalists, thinking it was quite a reasonable guess.

Next, I asked Liverpool Football Club to retweet my Parle flyer. Unfortunately, and irritatingly, they said they were not willing to help. I was less than impressed. I felt I hadn't been asking for the world – Liverpool had 11.6 million Twitter followers and I couldn't think of a better way of getting a lot of coverage and raising awareness of Parle's continued evasion of justice. If Liverpool didn't want to be linked with my campaign then they could arrange for an official police poster of Parle to be flashed up on the big screens inside the ground, either before the game or at half-time. With very little effort, I reckoned the club could have gone a long way towards creating one of the best opportunities ever to flush Parle out. I didn't think I was asking too much. I appreciated that the club were very busy in the week running up to the final and I guess my email probably wasn't top of their list of priorities. However, call me old-fashioned, but I think catching somebody who's wanted in connection with two murders is a bit more important than a football match. I sent chasing email after chasing email and, to their credit their media department did eventually get back to me before the day of the final, even if the response was in the negative.

I wondered if Merseyside police were putting plain-clothes spotters in the crowds in Madrid to potentially detect and arrest not only Parle, but other notorious Liverpool fugitives. Perhaps they were going to deploy mobile facial-recognition cameras? These have been the subject of heated debate because some regard them as an infringement of people's civil liberties – an attack on our freedoms – but I don't see it that way. Technology now helps the police in so many areas and the march of scientific progress simply cannot be stopped.

I'm convinced that, within a decade or so, every new CCTV camera that is deployed will use facial recognition. I think parliament has been very lax in its failure to debate the matter properly and to bring forward suitable legislation, but they have all been distracted by Brexit for so many years, and then by the coronavirus. If I had been leading the hunt for Parle as a detective, I would have liaised with the Spanish police and used facial recognition on the turnstiles or inside the stadium which, of course, would be absolutely smothered by CCTV. To this day, I don't know whether that happened, I suspect it did not, nor do I know if Parle went to the game or not.

Soon after the match a Spanish newspaper sent some photographs of a man who was tall, white and had a similar haircut to that of Kevin Parle, but certainly wasn't him. It looked like the paper was going to publish the photographs anyway, with the headline of, IS THIS KEVIN PARLE? I told them that I thought that was very unwise and they might end up hearing from this innocent man's solicitors at some point in the not too distant future. The game came and went. Liverpool won an awful game which I couldn't bring myself to watch all the way to the end.

The next day I listened to the recording of the conversation I'd had with Professor David Wilson. Among his many brilliant contributions was his dismissal of the idea that Parle might take a new identity. He felt this would be superficial – essentially, you end up playing at being somebody else – and he was convinced that Parle would not do that. I had adopted numerous different identities over the years when I was working undercover, once on a long-term basis during my catastrophic stint in the witness protection programme. As far as I was concerned, not only was the adoption of a new identity superficial, but I think it is unsustainable in the long term. I'm sure Parle gets off on having the respect of those around him: he'll want to be with people who will satisfy that need and he'll also need to be in an environment where the big man ego can thrive. I just had to find out where that was.

Spain was cropping up again and again. The Torrevieja sighting from 2006, reported in the media, seemed reliable, and other apparent sightings in Spain were coming my way, although none of them were particularly recent. A brand-new contact in the Costa Blanca called me on the burner phone to discuss a woman who was reputed in some circles to be the biggest cocaine dealer in the area. From the flimsy details I was given, my OSINT man Kyle was able to identify her and get some potential business addresses. She apparently knew Parle, although this information was little more than a rumour. But I have long thought that rumour is often truth's lubricant. It was tempting to get on a plane to the Costa Blanca, but I felt I needed something a bit more concrete. Besides, I'd spent the book payment a long time ago and the podcast was still not commissioned. Spain would have to wait: I could ill-afford to go splashing the family savings on a week in the sun.

There were other family complications. My wife came home one evening to find that she couldn't get in the front door because my worried teenage son had double-locked it from the inside. He explained, 'What if Kevin Parle pays us a visit?' I clearly had not allayed his fears when I'd had a chat with him and my wife was extremely unhappy about the impact the hunt was beginning to have on our family.

I'll take all the accusations about being selfish, but I wasn't going to chuck in the towel after just a few weeks or ever, in fact. In recent months my wife and teenagers have mentioned Parle less and less, although his name still reverberates around the house when I'm on the phone or giving a radio interview from my office. My wife and I went out shopping the other day and she said, 'Can we please just have one day where you do not talk about Kevin-bloody-Parle?' I'm very lucky to have the family that I do.

The fifteenth anniversary of Liam's murder was looming. I had plenty of unfinished enquiries in Liverpool and I wanted to lay some flowers in Grafton Street, where he had been gunned down. I thought it was important to acknowledge the anniversary and pay my respects. I reminded local media outlets that the anniversary was on the horizon – the Liverpool media has been, and continues to be, very supportive of what I'm trying to achieve. They understand that it has been impossible for me to sometimes tell them everything I know although, as journalists, they've wanted to know every little scrap of information that's in my head, my notebook or my laptop. In return, I have kept them in the loop whenever I can. I remain forever indebted to them. When Parle is found they can rightfully take a huge amount of credit.

This time I made the trip to Liverpool alone, with Mark due to join me the following day. He had a firm vision of how the storytelling would unfurl for the broadcast version and he sometimes wanted to interview contributors that would not take my investigation any further forward, such as journalists who had covered a relevant court case many years earlier. Sometimes, then, we went our separate ways, meeting up when the need arose. By this time Mark and producer Lewis had got a version of what we hoped would be the first episode ready and I took the opportunity to put on my headphones, relax back into my seat and press play. I was very impressed. My previous negativity around the podcast not getting commissioned vanished. I was convinced the BBC would want more of this.

I spent the rest of the journey mapping out the places we would visit and noting down the points that I wanted to get across in the media interviews. There were five main lines:

1. Courageous people were coming forward to speak to me. I wanted more of that please.
2. Spain and cocaine were increasingly being mentioned.
3. I'd been given the name of a criminal who may be currently linked to Parle.
4. The twenty-thousand-pound reward remains in place.
5. I appreciate that violence is often used as a currency within organised crime groups. I understand some people's concerns. I'll take the information and I'll take the risks, so the public don't have to.

Once I arrived at Lime Street station, I immediately made my way to the various media offices and spent the afternoon on the interview merry-go-round. Back at the usual hotel, I plotted the route Mark and I needed to follow the next day. Mark, fresh from his podcast travels, joined me at the hotel at about 11 p.m., just in time for a nightcap. A former colleague of mine, who was a Scouser, had contacted him to express their fears for my safety. They hadn't made these concerns known personally to me, because I expect they knew what my reaction would be. Poor old Mark copped it instead. I rode roughshod over the comments, even meant, as they were, in a helpful way.

'These people don't understand how society works,' I ranted. I got cranked up and approaching top speed as I fumed, 'Parle and the crooks that harbour him have to be more scared of what I'm doing than I am of them. The worst they can do is put a bullet in the back of my head, and if they do, so what? I've had a good life. In all likelihood I won't know very much about it. Let's face it, these sorts of people are not going to stoop to throwing a can of paint over my car are they, so bollocks to 'em. Can people just stop frigging worrying about me? I'm a grown-up, I'll take whatever comes at me.' I apologised to Mark for my outburst and bought him a drink.

Wednesday 19 June, 2019 was the anniversary. After breakfast Mark and I bought flowers and we made our way to Grafton Street. The skies were blue, the sun shone beautifully, but my mood was dark, very dark. I laid the flowers by railings opposite the spot where Liam had been executed and Mark, recording the moment, asked me how I was feeling. Emotions were racing around my head. My youngest son was now sixteen. Losing my precious baby at that age would simply destroy me. If somebody who was thought to be responsible for killing my boy was still at large fifteen years later, I could only hazard a guess at what that would do to me. I gave Mark the best answer I could. It would not provide the greatest broadcasting clip of my career. Bless you, Liam.

I left a pile of flyers alongside the flowers, with Liam's face pointing upwards. A resident came over for a natter. He told us he felt ashamed that he hadn't remembered it was the anniversary until he saw me. We did a pretty good job of assuaging his guilt. We took our time to stand and remember Liam.

We eventually got back in the car and I posted a picture on Twitter that Mark had taken of me laying the flowers. Very quickly people started to add likes and made very complimentary comments. I received an email from one of my merry band of helpers who had taken one of Parle's photographs and digitally altered it so that Parle was now seen smiling. I resisted the urge to post it immediately, because I felt it would have been highly inappropriate and insensitive and could have caused a lot of upset. I was itching to get it out there, but it would have to wait a little while.

Mark and I spent the rest of the day visiting addresses, many connected to the Parle family, and we didn't get an answer at a single one. We left flyers and business cards with a note written on the back. We headed back towards Grafton Street and I had to admit I felt a bit disheartened at the lack of response. I did get a message from the DCI, who wanted to know how we were getting on. I took that as a positive. Maybe some of the information I had passed to him did have some merit and he didn't regard me as just a pain in the rear end.

We visited Liam's old school and spoke to a wonderful lady who had worked there for many, many years and remembered Liam with some affection. Mark recorded an interview and we heard how the school had been vastly improved and renamed, and was widely regarded as a success story.

Mark had to head back south and I dropped him at Lime Street. I made my way back to the hotel, grabbed a bit of dinner and enjoyed a fairly early night. The next day, when I woke up and examined my phone, I saw the extent of the positive reaction there had been to the photo of me laying the flowers. I decided that I was going to post the altered photograph of the smiling Kevin Parle.

I visited a number of other addresses. Some of these were linked to the Parle family, and I did the usual, shoving flyers and business cards through letterboxes. I checked to find that not all the social media reaction to the photo of me laying flowers had been positive. One particular troll rather unflatteringly described me as an 'attention-seeking c**t'. Charmed, I'm sure.

The following day was Friday and I was due to travel home, but I woke up to the devastating news that a former colleague and friend had died. He'd been taken way too soon. He was a remarkable detective and I wondered to myself how many villains were still languishing in jail courtesy of his brilliant work, whether working undercover, kicking down doors, carrying out surveillance while remaining unseen or on many other kinds of operations. His death cast a shadow over my entire day.

More mundanely, my mobile was playing up and this only served to increase the concerns that I had about it potentially being hacked or bugged. Phone conversations would end abruptly and I couldn't hear what people were trying to say to me. I did the usual, turning it off and on again, but still it was unpredictable. I also realised I was getting through so much money, seemingly constantly having to visit ATMs. This was turning out to be a rather expensive venture, what with train fares, car hire, hotels and living away from home.

I dropped the hire car off and took a taxi back to the hotel. The driver was one of those warm, chatty, loveable Scousers. The conversation between us started with football, as it so often does. I discovered he was an Everton supporter who had very little time for Liverpool fans. He then asked me, 'What are you doing in Liverpool?' The moment I mentioned Kevin Parle he immediately snapped, 'He's a c**t.' He then told me that he'd known Lucy and, with emotion in his voice, described her as being as beautiful on the inside as she was on the outside. He continued, 'I'm telling you, she was a wonderful young woman.'

He'd once had some lads in the back of his cab when the police carried out an armed hard-stop on his vehicle: he was dragged out of the car at gunpoint, thrown to the ground face down and handcuffed, as were his passengers. He was released once the police understood he was an entirely innocent cab driver. His passengers, on the other hand, were dragged off into custody on account of the Uzi machine gun the police found on the floor in the back of the cab. I left the cab with the driver promising to call me if he heard anything about Parle.

I checked out of the hotel and decided that, as it was a rather lovely early Friday evening, I'd walk to the station. I ambled along and enjoyed listening to buskers who were in some cases good enough to be playing in front of a paying audience. Then there were others who crucified any tune they tried to play. People were beginning to gather outside the bars, music was pumping out including, of course, local lads The Beatles: I absolutely adore them. Lennon and McCartney wrote the soundtrack to my early years. I also love The Rolling Stones and many other performers, but The Beatles have a special place in my heart.

At Lime Street I sat outside having a fag, watching the world go by and waiting for my train. A group of four beautifully turned out women were standing in front of me. They were glammed up, ready for a night out on the town. One of them recognised me. She beckoned me over and we exchanged pleasantries. As always, I thrust flyers towards them, but one of the group swiftly raised her hand, palm facing me. In a rather sombre tone she said, 'I know exactly who you are and what you're doing. Beware of what you wish for. If you find him there will be a price on your head for the rest of your days.' On that rather sobering note I wished them well, said 'Goodbye,' and made my way into the station.

I detest shopping of any description, with the notable exception of a browse around a bookshop. That afternoon I'd treated myself to half an hour in Waterstones in the city centre, and I'd picked up a copy of *Fast Eddie: My Twenty Years on the Run as Britain's Most Wanted Man*, by Eddie Maher. I thought his book might give me some food for thought, so as soon as I was settled into my seat, I got stuck in. Mr Maher, a security guard, took part in the 1993 theft of a security van and its contents. He had driven off with £1.2 million in cash. Before the police could catch him, he'd bolted to the USA, where he lived until he was finally arrested in 2012. Fair play to him, he reinvented himself again and again, had a partner and a son, and adeptly managed to keep one step ahead of the authorities. That was until an aggrieved former daughter-in-law rumbled him and went to the police. He was returned to the UK and sentenced to five years in jail, serving half. This annoyed one of his former colleagues so much that he went to the media complaining about how Maher 'had got off lightly'.

If, like me, you enjoy true crime books, then I think it is a real page-turner, and I was in London before I knew it. To be honest, I did get a bit irritated with Maher's constant 'Woe is me, I was hard done by' tone, blaming everyone except himself for his travails, but don't let that put you off having a read. I'd give it a solid eight out of ten and Maher's exploits really got me thinking in relation to Kevin Parle. I made a list of questions based on what I'd read:

Will Parle speak a foreign language? He's a smart, intelligent guy. If he's been in Spain for years then I suspect the answer to that will be a resounding 'Yes'.

Will he always have an escape route planned, so he can bolt at short notice, should he ever get sight or sound of the authorities coming for him? I would do, if I were in his position.

Has he cut all links to his family back in Liverpool?

Is he such an utterly ruthless, self-centred, selfish and uncaring bastard that he could leave his own mum never knowing if he were alive or dead? That was a very difficult one for me to answer, seeing as the Parle family flatly refused to engage with me.

My thoughts turned from parallels with the Maher case to why Parle's family were not prepared to talk. Maybe they didn't want me to have the opportunity to ask them questions, to look into their eyes and come to a considered judgement of their answers. There may, of course, be a myriad of other, perfectly reasonable reasons why they didn't want to speak to me. What I do know is that they complained to the police that I was harassing them, as the DCI later told me. I completely refuted the suggestion. I'd paid a total of two visits to Parle's mother's house. I left a note and a business card and had absolutely no intention of returning. Other family members received one visit each from me. This did not remotely resemble harassment.

The police should have known if Parle had been in contact with his family. If I had been leading the police hunt I would have monitored every possible line of communication open to the Parle family – I'd have monitored, hacked, bugged and more, everywhere that they went, including cars, homes, workplaces. Now, I am not suggesting for one moment that any member of the Parle family was or is assisting their fugitive son or brother but, in the light of the publicity and interest generated by my hunt, I would argue that Parle may now be tempted to reach out to his family, if only to reassure them that he is alive.

Call me a dreamer – I'll take that on the chin. I understood the pressures and commitments that the police have these days and I appreciate that they have limited resources. I was very well aware of the workload that the DCI had, because he would often respond to my emails with, 'I'm now in charge of a new murder enquiry,' or, 'I'm in court with a murder trial.' However, Parle remains wanted for two ghastly murders and to quote that well-worn phrase often used by police, 'No stone must be left unturned.'

12

A GREEN LIGHT

It was just a week after the last Liverpool trip that Mark and I returned for a short visit on 28 June. I was getting disproportionately excited each time I went to the city, as my affection for the place grew and the number of Liverpool-based sources increased.

Mark broke the wonderful news that BBC Sounds – the corporation's streaming and download audio service – and BBC Radio 5 Live had commissioned a twelve-part series of our podcast. Needless to say, I was delighted. We would have a potential audience of millions and, as far as I was concerned, the world was going to shrink for Kevin Thomas Parle. And it was all thanks to Mark, that fantastic man now sitting next to me on the train. He had bought into the idea of working with me. He had arranged for us to pitch to the BBC bosses. And he had recorded the pilot episode that got the project over the line.

Mark had a clear vision for the structure of the podcast. The first six episodes would each have a central theme – the first two concerning Liam and then Lucy – with elements of my investigation woven around them. Episode three would relate my life experiences and delve into my motivation. The other shows in that first half would respectively focus on Parle, Liverpool and the experiences of other people who had spent time on the run.

The rest of the series would follow my investigation in real time. We would gather and record material, then edit and produce as quickly as we could. This was going to be the closest thing the audience would experience to following an investigation as it actually happened. Mark had secured the narrating services of the fabulously talented Sunetra Sarker, of *Brookside*, *Casualty* and *Ackley Bridge* fame. I'd watched *Casualty* with my family for years and I was very familiar with Sunetra's formidable acting talents. I thought her lilting Scouse tones and intonation would be brilliant. I was not wrong. Sunetra smashed it throughout the series. Mark also convinced multi-award-winning producer Lewis Borg-Cardona to become a crucial part of our very small team. Lewis operates at the very top of his game, as his trophy cabinet attests. He also did a remarkable job on the series.

Mark and I celebrated the big news with a slap-up cup of coffee from a motorway service area. For the first, but most definitely not the last time, Mark reminded me of my 'It'll never get commissioned', 11 p.m., red-wine-fuelled rant. That gag will run for as long as he and I remain friends, which I sincerely hope is until my dying day.

Then it was back to business. I filled Mark in on the information that I had received that week. There were not a lot of specifics on Parle, but I'd heard a considerable amount about the wider Liverpool criminality, particularly around drugs, guns and murders. Some crooks with delightful nicknames like 'One-Punch', 'Pancake' and 'Ice Bucket' all got a mention, but I wasn't going to do anything with this information. I certainly wasn't going to pass it to the police because it did not relate to my hunt for Parle. Some people came forward because they obviously thought I'd be interested in knowing about which unconnected person apparently shot which other random name but, frankly, I wasn't.

Mark and I headed for the part of Liverpool that was saturated with clubs and bars. I engaged with all the members of the city's door staff I could find; I had done some research that suggested some pretty lively people worked on the doors in the city. I am not one for generalising, but it is true that organised crime sometimes has a pretty tight grip on the security provided to entertainment venues, not just in Liverpool but in many cities of our great nation. The creation of the Security Industry Authority in 2003 by the Home Office did go some way to changing much of that; I speak from first-hand experience having, not so many years ago during challenging financial times, spent some time on the doors. I've met many of the people in that game. I know the drill. My maturity, life experiences and unwillingness to get physical with anyone (unless absolutely necessary), meant that, by and large, I had a good time and got paid for it. Thankfully, I was never assaulted. I did meet some security staff who were very quick to lay their hands on customers and some of these 'colleagues' were never going to get an invite to my house because I suspected they were connected to criminality.

The influence exercised by organised crime on the security industry has not completely disappeared, even today. But that wasn't a concern for Mark and I in our current guise – we were, not to put too fine a point on it, two tall, grey, old blokes. We stuck out like sore thumbs among the youngsters heading for a night out. This was exactly what I wanted. I could see the security staff disappearing off to get on their radios, their phones, or get face-to-face with colleagues to tell them what I was doing. Everybody got a flyer, whether they wanted it or not. Some of the staff were great. They nattered with us. Some shared a joke, some were helpful, and others not so. It was clear, though, that word was getting around. Good. Only one twat tried to play the big man and intimidate me, but I treated him with such disdain that I think he realised I was neither impressed nor intimidated by his antics. With the evening concluded, Mark and I treated ourselves to a couple of pints to round off the day.

The following morning I was up bright and early because I had a speaking engagement in the Merseyside Maritime Museum on the regenerated docks. I addressed an audience of cyber sleuths, open-source intelligence experts, ethical hackers and more. I didn't accept a fee for this gig. My reward would be the opportunity to win these twenty-first-century digital detectives over, and use them as more eyes and ears. Many were fascinated and intrigued by what I was doing. Some of them approached me with ideas and some had already done some online digging. To a technophobe like me, these were seriously scary people – by way of a demonstration, one of them hacked someone's phone, with their permission, in less time than it took the owner to enter their passcode.

The police had a presence at this convention. The North West Regional Organised Crime Unit was represented by their cyber crime team. I spent some time making friends with them, and they seemed very interested in my hunt. One of the officers went on to keep in touch with me and over the course of the day I learned a huge amount about ransomware (which can freeze a computer that can only be unlocked on payment of the ransom), hacking, online money-laundering, and how organised crime groups go about grooming and recruiting kids online. Having heard all of that I can only say, parents – please do not leave your kids in their bedrooms, online and unsupervised for hours on end. You have every right to know exactly what they're doing, so ask them. Some very serious criminals will be looking to ensnare your children into their criminality, with the lure of cash and more. And once they've achieved that, the lives of your youngsters could be blighted for ever.

I met an incredibly inspiring man who was on the autism spectrum. He had, quite remarkably, been able to use the condition positively. He now ran a recruitment agency that set out to find genius youngsters who lived their lives online and were in danger of joining criminal gangs and getting in trouble with the law. He represented large companies that wanted to employ these talented youngsters, many having the ability to hack a bank or a major corporation. Their role was to become poacher-turned-gamekeeper, advising these organisations on how to avoid being hacked or otherwise compromised, and in return they received a handsome salary and were able to set off down the pathway to a happy and fulfilling life on the right side of the law. The salaries mentioned to me dwarfed anything I could dream of earning. If you have a kid like that, get in touch, and I'll do my best to ensure the necessary introductions. After an enlightening few hours, I headed home.

I had a couple of holidays booked for July 2019. One was a lads-and-dads, five-day break in Center Parcs, a reward to my boys and those of my mates for working so hard for their school exams. It was also a great opportunity for the adults to consume industrial quantities of red wine while the youngsters were out doing their thing. It also provided me with the chance to tell my mates as much as I could about Kevin Parle. (No one escapes. I am officially the world's leading Kevin Parle bore, renowned for talking about him and the crimes he is wanted for, endlessly. Buy me a drink and ask me about him at your peril.)

The other holiday was with the family, taking a week-long break in the sun. Part of me was dreading the burner phone ringing during either trip; my wife and kids have had to suffer many holidays being interrupted by work over the years and let's just say they were not always thrilled. However, as I always do, I packed my work kit, comprising both personal and burner phone, notebook, pens and highlighters, handheld voice recorder and a stash of flyers. Even on holiday I carry them around with me, because you never know who you might get talking to at the beach bar. I'm always on duty, 24/7.

The holidays passed without disruption but, not long after returning from the second, I received a simple text message on the burner phone: 'Call me'. I did exactly that, and so began a journey that would make me question my abilities and my actions as I have seldom done before. This person didn't beat around the bush. They said they had seen Kevin Parle recently and that they would provide me with the information I needed to ensure that he was captured. But they also said they wanted to make a deal. Over a number of telephone conversations and texts, this man told me that he had suffered hugely at the hands of an organisation and wanted revenge. That would take the form of publicising what had happened to him. If I could do that, he promised me all the information I needed. This wasn't really in my power and it was clear he had an inflated idea of who I was and what I could achieve. I'm not a journalist for one of the national newspapers, much less for broadcast news. I made the limitations of what I could achieve perfectly clear, but I did say that I could probably arrange for a credible journalist from a national broadcaster to sit down and listen to his story.

Unusually, this man wasn't particularly fussed about the prospect of getting the reward from the police for Parle's capture and conviction. His main thrust was his need for publicity. We had an enormous number of telephone calls and it became clear he lived a rather chaotic life: sometimes conversations would be cut short and at other times he wouldn't be able to speak to me at all. I'll admit I was extremely keen to hear what he had to say about Parle and perhaps that blurred my judgement to some degree.

I certainly heard all the details of his own story. He showed me a considerable amount of paperwork that seemed to support some aspects and as he recounted what had happened to him he was very emotional and appeared credible. I arranged for him to come to London so that he could meet a journalist. This would also give me the opportunity to spend some time with this source, face-to-face, and hopefully I could get to know him better and make a more informed judgement call on the truthfulness of what he was telling me.

I got snippets of information about Parle before my caller arrived in London, including a physical description and a note of what he'd been wearing at the time of the sighting. He had also spoken to the fugitive, saying, 'I thought you were fish food.'

Parle apparently replied, 'I still am.'

To this day I think that's a great line. If I saw it in a TV drama, I would certainly think that was a creative, well-written snippet of dialogue. I certainly don't think I could write such a good line and insert it into one of my radio dramas. Perhaps I should give up that particular line of employment.

It's very difficult to find a cheap hotel anywhere in London and, as I was soon to discover when I booked two rooms, you get what you pay for. I arrived considerably earlier than the source and put my stuff in my room. I couldn't help but notice the frayed carpet on the stairs, the shabby décor, the shady faces going in and out of the hotel – I was extremely pleased that I hadn't booked this place for a weekend away with my wife. She would have gone absolutely ballistic, but for the investigation I had to keep an eye on costs. I'd decided to stay as well to squeeze as many hours as possible out of this short visit. I wanted to spend as much time in this man's company as I could. It was all done with the intention of trying to make a judgement call on whether I was being told the truth or not.

I'd done my research on this source and knew what he looked like. I took up a discreet position outside a café and, with a coffee in front of me, I saw him approach the hotel. The journalist who was to meet us had already arrived and I'd briefed her as best I could. She was waiting on a call from me at a nearby location.

I met my source in the basement restaurant that was otherwise completely deserted. I was keen to hear about what I regarded as the really important stuff – the where and when of this contact's encounter with Parle. These were the critical pieces of information that I needed, but my man was holding back until I got him what he wanted: publicity. Was this a very wise deal for me to enter into? Only time would tell. I thought I'd chance my arm and I asked the source where the sighting had been. He replied, 'Liverpool,' but wouldn't tell me any more. I didn't know whether to believe this or not, although there had been the reported sighting of Parle in the red Audi in Liverpool that I'd received only a matter of weeks before. Could what I was being told now really be true? I certainly wasn't going to dismiss it out of hand. I left the source and the journalist together for about an hour and he gave her his tale of woe.

We all met in my hotel room, where we were joined by Mark. The journalist went away to further research the story. She would get back to us. She took a copy of paperwork that the source had brought that appeared to corroborate his story. Mark had another meeting to disappear to, which left me and my source together, alone in the hotel room.

Once again, I probed the extent of his knowledge. He described Parle as scruffy, and said he had been wearing a baseball cap and sporting a ginger beard, which was quite long but trimmed. The cap was permanently on his head. The source went on to explain that Parle had a partner and they had a daughter together. The source suspected that the partner was completely in the dark about her partner's unsavoury past and most certainly didn't know that he was wanted in connection with two murders.

I drilled down on the detail in greater depth than I had over the phone. What kind of coat was Parle wearing? What kind of footwear was he wearing? How did he walk? Did he stand at his full height – six foot six inches? Each time I asked a question, the source instantly came back with a credible answer. I was building up a detailed description. However, the source still held back on where in the city it was that they met, and when. These two pieces of information were absolutely crucial.

I asked if Parle was aware that I was looking for him, which I guess was largely a vanity question on my part. The conversation was moved on swiftly by the source and I didn't get an answer. I should have probed that far more deeply. I asked if the source had seen Parle using a phone and if he had his number and if he knew where Parle lived. He said that he didn't know about a phone and insisted he wasn't going to tell me where he'd seen Parle because that would give a very big clue as to the area where he lived, and the source was holding those details back until I had fulfilled my part of the deal.

If ever you're speaking to someone and you are trying to establish whether they are being truthful or not, you can focus on certain matters that people find it very difficult to lie about. One area is the emotional; ask your subject how they felt at the particular time that they saw or otherwise experienced a particular event. Ask them to give direct quotes of any conversation – it's harder to make up dialogue than it is to be truthful. And be sure to question people about trivial details, irrelevancies. If someone can recall the minor things it is often a sign of their credibility. I did all that in this case and he seemed to come through. There was that line, 'I thought you were fish food,' and Parle's apparent answer, and descriptions of his own emotions. And he was able to give me details of what was going on around the two of them, like a conversation a couple of old boys were having close to him. And yet I still couldn't make my mind up as to whether this source was being truthful or otherwise. The exact where and when of the meeting with Parle was a very big carrot and he continued to dangle it. I desperately wished that I had alongside me an expert in telling truth from lies, someone who could make a dispassionate and objective judgement. I didn't, so I continued to bumble along doing the best I could. That evening he wanted to go out for something to eat without me and, again, I wonder if that should have rung alarm bells. Maybe, but I could fully understand this person not wanting to be seen in public with me. I do get recognised sometimes when I'm out and about, and I knew I could put him at risk.

My own cramped and far-from-luxurious hotel bedroom was not at all inviting and so I was actually quite pleased to find only one pubic hair in the bed as I pulled back the covers. The following morning we met again. I tested what he'd told me the previous day and his answers remained consistent. He taunted me yet again, saying the golden nuggets of information I craved would be coming my way once the journalist got a splash of publicity for the story he wanted to tell. We said our goodbyes. I made the police aware of the fact that I was in possession of information that Parle had been seen in Liverpool, adding that I didn't yet know when or where.

The source and I kept in regular contact and it would be fair to say he was pretty high-maintenance. From where I was sitting his life seemed quite chaotic. He made phone calls and texts at any time, including the early hours of the morning. At one point he pleaded poverty and said that he needed money in a hurry. By way of bank transfer I sent him £150. I don't have a lot of £150s to throw away and, for what it was worth, I very sternly instructed that the money was to be used only on essential living expenses rather than being squandered on alcohol or drugs. He promised it would only be spent on life's necessities. I was mindful that my relationship with his man could be held up to very close scrutiny in the future, especially if Parle was captured as a result of his information and he claimed the reward. I kept a ledger of every single penny that I spent on him, right down to the cost of a small bottle of water.

A couple of weeks later we arranged to meet again, this time with a new journalist – the first one had not run the story. Once again, I went through the whole routine of getting the budget hotel, meeting with the journo, and repeatedly asking the same questions of my source. He was adamant in restating the truthfulness of what he was telling me. Privately, I was still mentally tearing myself asunder, not knowing whether I was being led down the garden path.

There followed a frustrating three or four weeks during which we couldn't get a definitive answer as to whether or not his story was going to be run. Major national stories were dominating and other editorial decisions were being delayed or just not made at all. All the while, my source was on the phone bending my ear. He was not overly happy and to be frank, nor was I. But there was little or nothing I could do to alter the position we were in.

In the meantime, I was not only no nearer the information I needed from him but also had no way of knowing whether he was reliable. I even wondered if he'd undergo a lie detector test. The police would never dream of doing such a thing but I could because I really was at my wits' end in trying to find out the truth. I didn't know much about lie detectors and I thought the best thing to do was to give it a go myself. I contacted a lovely man called David Thompson who had founded Global Polygraph Solutions, widely regarded as world leaders in the field – 'polygraph' is another term for lie detector. David had previously enjoyed a magnificent career in the police, climbing through the ranks to become a senior and highly respected Scotland Yard detective. He had applied the highest standards throughout his policing career and now he did the same with his company, which was why they sat at the top of their specialised tree.

Lie detectors have been commonplace in US criminal courts for many years. Spending time with David was very enlightening, and I was surprised to learn how widely the test is used in the UK, even if it hasn't made it to our criminal courts. David was regularly asked to carry out internal investigations into company employees, espionage inquiries and background checks for people when they're applying for a job. Childcare disputes and domestic screening formed another part of his work, as potential nannies and other carers were scrutinised. Infidelity and marital disputes also led to the use of lie detectors. Such evidence has actually been admitted into British family courts, although not widely.

Despite their popularity, David described polygraph use as a grey area and he was absolutely right. There was no guarantee that the results would be entirely accurate. Intrigued, I asked him how a lie detector worked and he explained that a subject is asked a series of questions, having first had sensors attached to their chest, arms and fingers. These detect changes in breathing patterns, in heart rate and in perspiration levels. The resulting data is put through a very sophisticated algorithm that predicts the likelihood – if not to 100 per cent certainty – of whether or not the questions were answered truthfully or not.

There are a number of factors that can alter outcomes and these are quite complex. This uncertainty is, in part, the reason for the reluctance to allow the results into our criminal courts. It is a field of science that comes with an element of doubt. However, when the tests are conducted properly by a world leader such as David Thompson, and the environment is suitable, many people, particularly employers, do choose to rely on the results.

Lie detector results have been used in civil courts and tribunals to inform the overall evidence package. It has been known on rare occasions during criminal trials, where a defendant is, say, charged with rape and the issue in dispute is consent, for a sneaky defence barrister to weave a lie detector test result into the case by way of cross-examining the defendant, 'Did you undertake a lie detector test?' Once the jury have heard that, it is very hard for them to disregard it, even if they are instructed to do so by the judge.

I'm sure that lie detectors will be rolled out widely by the probation service, parole boards and the police with regard to deciding if sex offenders are suitable for release back into the community. I'm also sure there will be increasing use of them when convicted terrorists are assessed for release from prison. The questions they will probably be asked will relate to their feelings towards proscribed organisations.

David gave me a lot of his time for no charge whatsoever and I only had to pay for the test itself. By now we had received some money from the BBC for the podcast and a large chunk of that would be taken up with this research. But it was important to get it right: quite apart from trying to verify the information about the alleged sighting of Parle, the source had also told me that he was a friend of Anthony 'Fat Tony' Downes.

Yes, the same Tony Downes who had been tried and acquitted of Lucy's murder, alongside Kirk Bradley. And my source had an astonishing allegation to make about Fat Tony.

13

FAT TONY

Tony Downes and Kirk Bradley had become infamous since their acquittal for Lucy Hargreaves' murder. Downes went on to be sentenced to seven years in jail for a series of ATM thefts. While incarcerated in prison he continued to plot and plan crime.

Downes and Bradley, during 2009 and 2010, were among a number of people who conducted a campaign of terror across the city of Liverpool. This involved shootings and the use of grenades to destroy property. One such grenade was mistakenly placed on the garden wall of the Liverpool Football Club legend Kenny Dalglish, when it had been intended for someone else entirely. Fortunately, that weapon did not explode.

Downes and Bradley described themselves as blood brothers. They were both quite shrewd in distancing themselves from the shootings and the explosions, but eventually enough evidence was gathered about these puppet-masters to prosecute them for their epidemic of violent lawlessness. The gang members that Downes and Bradley ruled over used scrambler bikes so they could attack and disappear in double quick speed. They favoured Luger

Browning semi-automatic pistols, and their grenades were packed with ball bearings and shrapnel. Between 2009 and 2011, Downes and Bradley were responsible for sixteen shootings and four grenade attacks. In one, a grandmother and a young child had to run for their lives. In another, a paramedic – the victim of mistaken identity – was shot in his own home. Another victim had to have a leg amputated after being shot while in a phone box and another victim received a bullet in the stomach outside a wake at a pub in West Derby, Liverpool.

During their trial, Downes and Bradley were transported from remand centre to court by prison van until, in week eleven, just after 8.30 a.m. on 13 July 2011, it was targeted by a gang of masked men. One of the guards was dragged from the van and beaten severely while a man shouted at the driver, 'Get the fucking keys out or I will blow your fucking head off.' Downes and Bradley were bundled into a white Saab that was discovered abandoned later. Their escape enraged local Walton MP, Steve Rotherham, who criticised the prison authorities for letting two such dangerous prisoners get away. The elaborate and brutal escape plot had been hatched by Downes from inside jail, using an illicit mobile phone which had been monitored by the authorities: they were gathering evidence against him about other offences.

Somebody told me who funded that prison van breakout, how much it cost, who paid their fair share of it and who didn't. That information is for me to know and nobody else to find out. It is one part of all the information I received that was unrelated to my hunt for Parle. It will for ever remain locked in my head. The *Liverpool Echo* later declared that this prison van escape cost the taxpayer £300,000 because the trial had to be abandoned. Rather surprisingly, nobody has ever been prosecuted in connection with that audacious breakout and I frequently ask myself, why not?

Downes and Bradley both fled the UK. Downes was recaptured in March 2012 in a small holiday city called Goes, in the Netherlands, close to the border with Belgium. He was travelling in a car when it was surrounded by a team of Dutch armed police and was returned to the UK, while the hunt for Bradley continued. A new trial was ordered, and this took place in Woolwich Crown Court in south London – clearly, it was too risky to hold their trial once again in the north-west. There were a number of other men charged with very similar offences that were connected to Downes and Bradley's work as the ringmasters.

Bradley himself was arrested a month later in Amsterdam. Police smashed through the door of the flat where he was living and, by all accounts, Bradley was extremely surprised to see them; he was pictured in handcuffs, wearing flip-flops and shorts, while being firmly restrained by a member of the Dutch law enforcement forces in a balaclava.

Downes and Bradley were both found guilty and the judge sentenced the pair of them to life imprisonment with a minimum term of twenty-two years each. Gary Wilson, a twenty-seven-year-old man from Southport, was sentenced to life with a minimum of sixteen years. Craig Riley, twenty-five, of Stockbridge Village, was sentenced to life with a minimum of fourteen years and Joseph Farrell, twenty-three, of Knowsley, was given a minimum sentence of twelve years. When describing Bradley, the judge said, 'He is plainly a very dangerous man. Any right-thinking member of the public would feel abhorrence and outrage at this merciless campaign which Bradley oversaw and co-managed.'

Downes' and Bradley's blood-brother relationship didn't last long after they'd been sent down: in November 2012, Downes attacked Bradley with a weapon that he'd manufactured in Belmarsh prison. Bradley was not seriously hurt but they had to be separated by prison staff.

And now, in 2019, the man who had already claimed to have seen Parle, who had taken up so much of my time, efforts and emotions, had something truly astonishing to say. He alleged that Anthony Downes had made a full and frank confession to him about his part in Lucy's brutal murder. The source went on to confirm that this 'confession' was made after Downes and Bradley had been acquitted of Lucy's murder. This information, if true, was potentially evidential gold. I probed the source at length, and he later provided details of the location and a timespan over which he maintained this 'confession' by Downes took place. The reason it could be so important was because of the partial abolition of what had been known as the 'double jeopardy' rule.

For more than eight hundred years it had been a rock-solid principle of British law that no one can be tried for the same crime twice – which was absolutely right. If the state accuses you of a crime and fails to prove their case, then they should not be allowed to come back and have a second or even a third go: that would be persecution, not prosecution. In the main, the double jeopardy rule does still apply in the UK, but the Criminal Justice Act of 2003 created some exceptions, where 'fresh and compelling evidence' is discovered, and even then further action can only be taken under the authority of the director of public prosecutions. In these very limited cases, somebody can be tried twice.

This change in the law largely came about thanks to the dedicated work and campaigning of the mother of twenty-two-year-old Julie Hogg, who had been murdered in 1989. Ten years later a man called William Dunlop confessed to her murder to a prison officer, but he could only be charged with perjury (having lied at his previous trial) and not murder because he had previously been tried and found not guilty of that heinous crime. This was, of course, a ludicrous situation.

Since the law has been changed there have been some rare cases in which people have stood trial for a second time, most notably Gary Dobson, once acquitted of the racist murder of the young black man, Stephen Lawrence, in south London in 1993. Nearly twenty years later, in 2012, he was eventually convicted of that abominable crime.

And now my source had made a similar allegation relating to Anthony Downes. If this alleged 'confession' could be proved, it could be absolutely explosive. I ruminated long and hard, once again, about what I should do with this information. I'd taken countless statements from important witnesses during my time in the police and I wondered whether or not I should meet up again with the source, sit down, thoroughly debrief him and take a statement detailing the allegation about Downes, so that I could then present the statement to the police. The only reason I even contemplated doing this was because the source had absolutely no time whatsoever for the police and spoke about them in the most disparaging way.

This course of action would be fraught with danger, and quite possibly extremely irresponsible. I was not up to speed with current police procedures for statement-taking, let alone tackling long, complex and potentially very important allegations, upon which a court case about one of the country's most horrific unsolved crimes might hang. I could imagine the DCI's face if I pitched up with such a statement. I was pretty sure he'd find a smile rather hard to come by.

I also had to consider that the entire tale of this alleged 'confession' being made by Anthony Downes could be entirely untrue. But, if that was the case, then what would be the reason for the source to lie? He was desperate for me to be a gateway to the publicity he craved. Would he invent all the information about the Parle sighting, the conversation, and the 'confession' by Downes, merely to sucker me in, get his story into the press and then deny everything or break off all contact? My head was spinning as I tried to make some sense of it all. As someone who has always regarded himself as a half-decent investigator, I'll admit, I was wrestling with this one, and not winning.

If the Parle information was a complete concoction, designed to waste my time, make me part with my money and just look foolish, I could handle that. I had long suspected that those with Parle's best interests at heart might launch such a stunt. What I found much harder to accept was the idea that somebody might fabricate a confession that could raise the hopes of some sort of justice for Lucy's ghastly murder, a crime of almost unparalleled wickedness. The source had admitted to me that he had experienced mental health struggles – as have I. I understand that. This is why I often speak publicly about the importance of good mental health and the need for sufficient services for those with their challenges. I owe my life to brilliant mental health workers. But the creation of a false confession about such a terrible crime? That could only come from the mind of a seriously evil person.

I was going to have to rely on the police for some kind of a concrete steer. So much was hanging on this information.

While protecting his identity, I passed the information on to the police and I waited … and waited. By now it was the middle of September 2019 and the DCI contacted me to tell me that Parle would feature on an upcoming edition of the BBC's *Crimewatch Roadshow* programme. Needless to say, I was glued to my TV and watched with enormous interest. The audience was told that Parle was wanted in connection with Liam's murder but there was no mention of him being wanted for Lucy's murder. I found that rather strange and wondered whether the police, in light of the acquittal of Downes and Bradley, now thought it unlikely that Parle would ever be convicted of that crime. I was pretty sure that the police hadn't had the time to check the veracity of the alleged 'confession' by Downes to the source.

Another couple of weeks passed and my frustrations grew. The second journalist had also not appeared very keen to publish the source's story, although I could understand their reasons. This source had a chequered background. Much of what he was telling the journalists was difficult to corroborate. As I relayed the bad news back to the source he became increasingly irritated. He wasn't the only one. I was not pleased that he was holding me to ransom by not giving me the last pieces of the information about Parle, which, if true, could be a game-changer.

On a much brighter note, the BBC wanted to meet with me and Mark and we drove up to Manchester, staying in a hotel overnight so that we would be in the BBC's Media City bright and early. Unfortunately, not long after we'd arrived in Manchester I got a phone call to tell me that my dear friend Roy had died of a heart attack. I'd known him since we were teenagers. He was younger than me, had two beautiful daughters and an amazing wife, all of whom were utterly devastated at his sudden and shocking death. A dark cloud hung over our visit.

That night we had a meeting with Chris Warburton, a Radio 5 Live presenter. Mark and Chris had previously created a fabulous, award-winning podcast called *Beyond Reasonable Doubt?*, which told the story of the death of Kathleen Peterson in the USA in 2001. There was a great deal of controversy surrounding the case, much of which still rages today. The podcast had rightfully done extremely well for all concerned, and I strongly recommend you have a listen. I did my best to be decent company with the other two. We had beer and enjoyed a meal but, inside, my heart was breaking for Roy and his family.

The following morning the meeting with the BBC went really well. We met the senior management of Radio 5 Live, along with representatives of their digital department, marketing, press and others. There was an enormous amount of energy and enthusiasm for the podcast. Everyone we met now knew about Kevin Parle and wanted him caught. Someone had created some fabulous artwork for the project, the PR was going to ramp up some publicity, and it really felt like we had the weight of the organisation behind us. I was delighted. I was confident that a huge new audience was now going to hear about Liam, Lucy and Kevin Parle. This would be an audience that I most definitely wouldn't have reached any other way.

Mark and I left Media City and headed west to Liverpool, where I again met with the source. By now I had paid for his hotel twice and shelled out for his train journeys, in addition to the £150 I transferred into his bank account. If he wanted to meet me again it would have to be on my terms – in Liverpool and during the next couple of days. He agreed to come to our hotel where I explained that I still didn't have a definitive decision on his own story. I was upfront and truthful about the two journalists he'd previously met.

This made him extremely unhappy and he had a temper-tantrum but then, in an outburst that I felt came more out of exasperation than anger, he blurted out the last pieces of the jigsaw: the name of the pub at which he and Parle had apparently met, the date and time, and the location of his child's school, which he allegedly walked to every day. The source stormed towards the hotel room door, but I managed to convince him to stay for a bit so we could continue our chat. This gave me an opportunity to test these latest snippets – or would they prove to be golden nuggets? To tell the truth, doubts about him still lingered, but now was the time for action.

We eventually parted, leaving Mark and I alone in the room. I chronicled every piece of the source's information about Parle in my A4 notebook, totalling sixteen items. If they were true, I was entirely confident they could lead us to capture Parle. I now had times, dates and locations, and a full description of how Parle apparently now looked. What could possibly go wrong? Fifteen of these points were written in black ink. The sixteenth point I wrote in red. The source said that he thought Parle would be carrying a gun. He hadn't seen a gun and such a weapon had not been discussed between them, but the source was sure himself that Parle would be armed. It might only be a suggestion, but Mark agreed that my hands were tied and I had to do the right thing having heard talk of a gun, which was to pass this information immediately to Merseyside police. I rang the DCI and we were invited to meet him the next day in the same swanky, modern building that we had visited a few weeks earlier.

Mark and I treated ourselves to a bit of dinner and bottle of wine that night and needless to say, the conversation was dominated by the question, 'Is this truth or is this lies?' and, frankly, neither of us could be certain. The following morning, we were ushered up to the same meeting room. The DCI said, 'Judging by the urgent tone in your voice yesterday, I thought you might have Parle in the boot of your car.' I gave the detectives a full rundown of my relationship with the source and I handed them all of the information. Back in the car I told Mark that if this had been the 1980s or the 1990s, and the information was truthful, I'd expect Parle to be sitting in a cell in about thirty-six hours, maybe a little bit longer.

I regaled Mark with the story of how I found a fugitive called James Alexander Baigrie, way back in March 1985. Baigrie, who had been serving a life sentence in a high-security prison in Scotland for shooting dead a publican during a robbery, carried out an extremely audacious escape. He was firmly at the top of Scotland's most-wanted list. Officers hunting for him had carried out an exhaustive search at the home of his best friend. They had taken the place apart, floorboard by floorboard, wall by wall, and had found nothing of interest whatsoever, except for a tiny, crumpled scrap of paper with a London telephone number on it.

A subscriber check on the number led to an address in Earl's Court, London, which was on the patch of Kensington police station where I was working in the CID office. I could hear the colleague who received the call about the information and it all sounded extremely interesting. This colleague was less experienced and, dare I say it, less streetwise than me, so I made it my business to find out exactly what was going on. We soon discovered that the address was an enormous, four-

or five-storey, terraced house that once would have been home to a very wealthy family and their staff. It had long since been converted into flats and bedsits. My colleague identified the room where a man who might match Baigrie's description was said to be living. We made a plan to raid his room at first light the following day.

At 5 a.m. a DS and I each booked out a gun from the station sergeant's safe. It was agreed that I would be first through the door, as I invariably was whenever we did a search. I was a headstrong and fearless young thing back then. With a Smith & Wesson revolver in my hand, I booted in the door of one of the bedsits and steamed into the room, shouting, 'Armed police.' I saw two single beds, only one occupied. I hollered at the young man to whom I'd given a very rude awakening, to slowly get out of bed. With my finger on the trigger and my gun pointed firmly at his chest, I was more than ready to deal with any non-compliance with my orders. He meekly did what he was told.

We questioned him at length about the person who usually slept in the other bed. We were spun a yarn about this flatmate, who we were told was a lovely bloke and had gone out for a drink the previous evening and not returned home. This was apparently a common occurrence. This kid wasn't going to harm a fly, so I put my gun back into my shoulder holster and set about having a nose around the room. I found a photograph of a man that bore some resemblance to the mugshot that we had of Baigrie but my colleagues and I were all far from convinced we were looking at the same person. I sneakily pocketed the photograph, intending to send it up to Scotland on the first flight I could, so that the cops up there could give us some indication as to whether or not it was Baigrie.

Outside the flat, some of my colleagues left to go and get some breakfast, including the sergeant with the other gun. But I was a very inquisitive detective. I was sure I'd heard that Baigrie might be labouring and, while my colleagues chatted, my attention was held by a builder's van on the other side of the road. Call it a copper's hunch, a sixth sense or downright nosiness, I went over and had a look. I checked the tax disc, noticed there was a partition between the front and rear of the Transit-type van, and walked around to the back. Please note, I did not check the tyres (that's what traffic cops do, not detectives).

There was a window in each of the two rear doors and I tried to peek in, struggling to get a clear view through the dirt and the gloom; all I could make out was what appeared to be just the sort of junk you might find in the back of an untidy builder's van. I tried the rear door handle and to my surprise it was unlocked. Never one to pass up such an opportunity, I clambered in. A head immediately popped up from under a grubby blanket.

I dug inside my jacket in an effort to draw my revolver and blurted, 'Good morning, I'm an armed police officer,' and found myself staring down a double-barrelled, sawn-off shotgun a few inches from the end of my nose. This was no time for heroics: in the finest traditions of the Met, I legged it, shouting, 'He's got a fucking gun!' to my startled fellow detectives. They all scarpered as fast as their legs would carry them, except for one colleague who once again entered the house to 'have a little word' with the young man who had obviously been less than truthful with us just a few minutes earlier.

I kept running away in an effort to avoid being blasted to death in the back, at last diving to safety behind a parked car some twenty feet from the van. I started to yell lies at the top of my voice. I told Baigrie he was surrounded by armed police and that he had no option but to surrender. I could see him moving around in the back of the van, and fully expected him to come out blasting his shotgun at all and sundry. I was scared for the public who were setting off for work. I was scared for my unarmed colleagues. I was so glad I had a gun. I braced myself for a very messy and challenging shoot-out.

Fortunately, Baigrie believed all my nonsense about being surrounded and stayed put. After what seemed like an eternity, the firearms branch arrived, laden with heavy weaponry, and I was allowed to wriggle out of the prone position that I'd been maintaining now for a couple of hours. I clambered out from underneath the car that had kept me hidden, while Baigrie stayed in his van for nearly forty-eight hours. The siege caused traffic chaos for miles around and made front-page headlines. Eventually, he turned the shotgun on himself and blew his brains out. Mark was gripped by the story and later weaved it into the podcast series.

The two of us continued to connect tirelessly with people who would help me with my hunt for Parle, bring experiences or expertise to the podcast, or both. We travelled across Liverpool to meet a man who assured us he was a reformed criminal, but nonetheless retained some pretty useful contacts. I didn't care about his background – I was ready to speak to absolutely anyone who might help. I was in no rush. I was in this for the long haul if need be.

We passed close to Crosby beach, the home of Antony Gormley's remarkable statues that form the piece of work *Another Place*. One hundred, life-size, iron statues are positioned across the beach, all of them looking out towards the sea. I had visited this truly evocative and moving installation some years earlier with my family, when we made one of our regular visits to see my eldest son at university. On that occasion it had been a lovely bright and crisp day.

On this day, however, it was pissing down. Mark had never seen the statues and, as we had about half an hour until our next meeting, he decided to brave the weather and take a look – there's no fool like an old fool. I stayed in the car writing emails and making phone calls. Mark returned some time later, drenched and with mud and sand covering him from his boots to his knees. He related a tale of woe involving quicksand or something but, quite frankly, I wasn't paying much attention. As far as I was concerned, he only had himself to blame. Not that I loved him any less for it. He soon changed his footwear and, as always, drove us to the next rendezvous.

We were heading to a coffee shop and when we parked I tried to get Mark – as I always did – to leave the nose of the car facing outwards from any car parking space, in case we had to make an exit a bit sharpish. This was a habit that harks back to my old days working undercover and it remains something I do each time I park, without fail. Some habits just never leave you.

We were meeting with a baseball-cap-wearing, track-suited man. From what I'd seen recently it appeared to be a very popular look in certain parts of Merseyside. I could never carry it off. In the hour or so that followed, I didn't get any specifics on Parle, but we were regaled with some stories that I can only describe as delightful – such as that of the human head of a murder victim being microwaved to prevent blood seeping from it. That was particularly interesting, although I have no way of knowing if it were true or not, and as it did not relate to my hunt for Parle I wasn't overly interested.

My ears pricked up when this man talked of a large Scouse community in Perth, Western Australia. This connected with something I already knew: in February 2016 many media outlets had run the story of a man who was convinced that he had had a drink with Parle in a Perth waterside bar. The reports were a bit light on detail; they didn't contain any quotes from Parle, for example, or make mention of anything that was discussed between this alleged witness and the man he believed was Parle. The police commented that they had 'credible information', but did not elaborate further. Apparently, it had been this sighting that had encouraged Merseyside police and the National Crime Agency to ask John Moores University to produce computer-altered pictures of how they thought Parle would look ten or more years on from the murders he was wanted for. It was these pictures that I used on my own flyers.

Australia is a line of enquiry that I haven't particularly pursued, yet. It remains on my radar, but my hunt has received quite a bit of publicity down under and I would like to think I might have received a snippet or two if he was holed up down there, yet I have not received any information whatsoever to indicate that might be the case. I am not pouring cold water over this sighting in any way, as I spoke to one person who told me that one of Parle's brothers had gone to Australia on holiday and returned in what is best described as a miserable frame of mind. Apparently, there is a family connection to that part of the world.

Before we left the source in the cafe, I asked how he thought Parle would behave when he is found and arrested. 'It will get messy,' was his chilling response. I was also utterly convinced that this man knew a lot more than he was willing to tell us.

We spent a considerable amount of time on this trip visiting Parle's primary and secondary schools in the leafy, well-heeled south of the city. We saw the big, posh houses of Mossley Hill, drove past Penny Lane, the street made famous by The Beatles song of the same name, and marvelled at Liverpool College, the private institution that Parle had attended. It looked resplendent, with three rugby pitches, grand architecture and air of academic achievement. We also saw what was obviously a drug deal go down just around the corner.

14

MALE DETAINED

Back at home the days crept by. I was longing for a call or an email from the DCI. My rampant impatience got the better of me and I fired off an email. I got a fairly prompt response saying that 'the information is being developed and as such, there is nothing further to add at this time'.

I reminded myself that I was not going to be put in the picture about everything they were doing and that I had to live with that frustration but, eventually, I did decide to take matters into my own hands. A great friend who I have known for decades, since we used to work together on drugs cases, had always supported me in my hunt for Parle and didn't live very far away from Liverpool. He was vastly experienced in surveillance and I brought him into the fold, sending him the list with my sixteen key pieces of information. He happily volunteered to go and do a reconnaissance of the area that we were told Parle had used, including the school to which he apparently walked his daughter every day. My mate had no concerns about being able to work covertly – there were plenty of places where he could mingle and hang around with other members of the public, including a bus stop and a number of shops.

On 16 October he told me he would be on the plot early the following morning, in time to see the kids arrive for school. I was due to meet my agent at the same time and, indeed, my mate called me as I was on my way, reporting his sighting of a man walking a small child to the school in question. He said this man was a 99 per cent match for the description of Parle, as related by the source. The baseball cap, the coat, the beard, the stooped walk and the child herself all matched. My mate had also seen pictures of Parle in the media over the years and while there was now a marked difference, he still felt it could actually be him.

My agent was picking me up from the station. I had arrived early, had a few minutes to wait and dived into a coffee shop. My heart was pounding. I was trying to process what I'd just been told. Could my mate really have just seen Kevin Parle in Liverpool? I desperately wanted this to be true. I was wishing the time away until I was able to use the privacy of my agent's car to call Mark and the police. I grabbed a coffee and another for my agent and paced up and down outside the station. I smoked one cigarette after another until she arrived. I leapt into her car and gave her an update. Now there were two of us who were rather excited. I rang Mark. Now there were three. I next brought the DCI up to speed. He asked to speak to the former colleague who had carried out this surveillance, which was fair enough. Once I'd squared it with my mate, I sent his number to the DCI. We both had meetings to go to and agreed to speak later on that day.

The DCI and certain sections of the Merseyside police moved swiftly to launch an operation for the next day. I asked if I could travel up to witness proceedings from a safe distance. By now it was late afternoon and the train was an unlikely option; I needed to go home, pack an overnight bag and get back into central London. I was, however, more than willing to drive through the night, collecting Mark on the way. If this was to be the moment Parle was captured, I really didn't want to miss it. But the response from the DCI was a firm 'No'. I was not happy about that. The police are forever having documentary and news crews following them around. Why couldn't Mark and I be sat in the back of a police van, at a place of their choosing, so we might just catch a glimpse of Parle in handcuffs?

I only slept a handful of hours and was up at the crack of dawn, pacing up and down my lounge. I had a coffee and a fag on the patio. And then another … and another. Eight o'clock came and went … 8.30 a.m., and then 9 a.m. This was proving to be the longest morning of my life. At 9.43 a.m. I received a text message. 'Male detained. It is definitely not KP. Update you later'. I slumped into my armchair, stared at the wall, and muttered a fair few expletives. I rang Mark and my agent. I was crestfallen.

A couple of cups of coffee later, I'd picked myself up, largely dusted myself down and decided that I needed to move on quickly from this extremely disappointing outcome. I spoke to the DCI later that day and tried to call the source. There was no answer and I sent him a message to the effect of, 'Why did you lead me on?' Soon afterwards I received a string of text messages littered with abuse. It was blatantly obvious that any relationship I may have had with that source was now firmly dead and buried.

I never got the opportunity to fully debrief him, to find out what his motives were for making such a fool out of me. I could have made a pretty good guess though. A couple of days later I had another string of texts, once again abusing me and saying that, due to the breakdown in trust between the two of us, he was going to go to a TV production company and another investigative journalist, and that the prize of Kevin Parle would be theirs. 'Good, fuck right off, you complete time-waster', was my attitude. I can live happily, even after being mugged off. I put myself up for people to take a pop at and I've only got myself to blame. Fair play to anyone involved in the conception and the practice of this deception on me, you got me fair and square. You had your moment of glory. But I've learned so much from that period and I thank you for the lessons it taught me. Time will eventually show your move up for being an own goal of monumental proportions, for the whole episode has given me more experience and the resolve to never, ever give up on my hunt for Kevin Parle.

The only conclusion I can now draw is that not only was the Parle 'meeting' and 'information' a yarn, but that the Anthony Downes 'confession' to Lucy's murder was the wicked concoction of a severely twisted mind. Needless to say, I haven't been contacted by any TV production companies to give my opinion on this source. I'm sure I would have been if he'd ever really found anyone to take him on. My name is now synonymous with Parle and they would have spoken to me as part of their due diligence.

A couple of weeks later, the DCI asked to be put in contact with my informant. I suspected that he probably wanted to fully debrief this utterly discredited source about the 'confession' allegedly made by Anthony Downes. Well as far as I was concerned, he could have him, with my very best wishes. I had no intention of engaging with him ever again. But the show must go on. We had a BBC podcast series to make, I had this book to write and there was a fugitive to be found. There was a lot to be optimistic about. Various sources in Spain were contacting me. One told me that Parle had been seen drinking in a bar called Chillout, in a small town not far from Benidorm called Albir. This sighting had apparently taken place within the last twelve months.

Another source, on the Costa Blanca, had been following my hunt and was having a conversation with someone about it, when another person abruptly interrupted: 'You'd better stop talking about Kevin Parle because he is the kind of man who can stop your conversations if you don't.' This source reported back to me a few days later, admitting they had been terrified by this intervention and would not be discussing the subject ever again. I could not afford to ignore Spain any longer.

It was stories like that which were causing me deep concern and I continued to be plagued by self-doubt. I felt that any ability I might have had to sort the wheat from the chaff, truth from lies, had abandoned me. I wondered whether the hunt for Parle was now massively backfiring. Had the publicity that I had gained merely served to increase his reputation? Could decent people now be intimidated for merely talking about him? Had newfound notoriety and reputation transformed Parle's name into some form of currency for criminals to trade on, as they sought to frighten people into keeping silent, or forced people into doing what they wanted them to do? Had I inadvertently made him more feared by the good people, and more revered by the bad people?

I hadn't anticipated or even considered this possibility when I'd started out. I was now questioning every move I made and becoming increasingly concerned on a daily basis. Not for the first time I had to remind myself, sternly, about why I was doing this. This was about Liam and Lucy. This was about truth over lies. This was about the need for an accused man to stand in a court and answer for his actions.

Mark was putting together the first few episodes of the podcast and sent me two clips from BBC's *Crimewatch* which related to Lucy's murder. The first was from May 2006, when the show was presented by Nick Ross and Fiona Bruce, and featured a reconstruction that was a very emotional piece of television. Not only did we see clips of Lucy's happy childhood, her dancing and her being the very epitome of a girly-girl, but we saw the DCI who started the investigation, Ian Mulcahey, standing in the scorched hallway of Lucy's burnt-out house. He spoke about the intensity of the fire, which was clear to anybody watching the show. He mentioned a white van that had been parked near her home in Lambourne Road, and that the driver had sat in the vehicle for ages. The police wanted to know who he was, and what he had seen. We were told about a petrol can that was filled at a petrol station. We were also told that Lucy's front door was forced open and that the three men wearing balaclavas entered the house. Two blasts from a full-length barrelled shotgun. The reconstruction was horrific and showed what a ghastly and appalling crime Lucy's murder had been. Apparently, someone phoned police from a telephone box, 'I know the lads that have just done it.'

I didn't hear any more from the police about the possibility of speaking to Anthony Downes. As far as I was concerned, the source who had given up the allegation was entirely discredited, and the alleged 'confession' could not be relied upon in any way, shape or form. However, I still wanted to talk to Downes, not only to give him the chance to tell me what he thought about the allegation, but also to ask whether he had any information on Kevin Parle. I knew it was a very long shot, but I've always believed that fortune favours the brave and, besides, I had nothing to lose.

I submitted an application to find out where he was serving his sentence. It was HMP Frankland, Durham and I asked him if he would allow me to visit. To his credit he took the time to write back. This is what he said – the asterisks represent text that was blacked out by the prison authorities. You can guess what the original said:

Dear Mr Bleksley

I have just received a letter from you regarding a book and podcast series you are doing in the search for Kevin Parle. I don't know why you are searching for Parle when you don't know the facts of what Mr Parle is allegedly on the run for. He is certainly not on the run for the Hargreaves murder as the trial judge, H. H. J. Henry Globe, stated in his closing speech, 'If Mr Parle was in the dock he would also be proven innocent and found not guilty.' But you people … don't act on facts, you act on gossip. However, Mr Parle is living in a shed in my mum's backyard, but will you keep that between me and you? Because some ****** thinks he in Spain fixing washing machines, what a ****.

You just missed him in the Champions League game, he was the mascot, but he only stayed for the first half as he had a washing machine to fix. If you pop around to me mum's to look in the shed, his favourite meal is Nando's, will you bring him one? He'll appreciate that.

I would be very grateful if you didn't mention me in your book or your podcast series. You are embarrassing yourself with the crap you're coming out with. I don't know whether you are looking for publicity or attention, but I think you should stick to ****** off celebrities and make a series of how you caught them because it's clear you're not very good at looking for criminals, especially with your 'trusted sources'.

I would also like to say, why the hell would I let you visit me? Do I have a visit from some **** from *Celebrity Hunted* or my family? Don't insult me, you gobshite. Please don't try and write back as you'll now be removed from my correspondence sheet. Keep embarrassing yourself,

Tony Downes

There were further attempts to dissuade me. Mark said that he'd been contacted by a man who had walked away from his previous life of crime in Merseyside but was still well connected with many villains. The source warned Mark, 'You had better call it off.' There was and is no chance of that ever happening.

There was a more positive development when I heard from ITN Productions, who make TV shows for a number of broadcasters. They had been commissioned by a channel called CBS Reality to make a ten-part documentary series to be called *New Scotland Yard Files*. This would showcase the great work that detectives had done in solving a number of murder cases. ITN were sounding me out for a presenting role and, after a number of meetings, I was confirmed as the frontman. I was delighted; the work would add some welcome cash to the family pot and, as I hadn't been a presenter before, this would be a new challenge. I would learn new skills and it might be good for my profile, because the more people that recognised me from the media, the more people would learn about Kevin Parle. I was also able to continue to prioritise my hunt for the fugitive, as the show only required a couple of weeks' filming. Most of it was done in the depths of winter, and it was absolutely freezing, but luckily I still had plenty of thermal underwear from way back in my bodyguarding days.

Information about Parle continued to come in. Periodically, articles were still appearing in the press, particularly the *Liverpool Echo*. Mark and I would regularly meet or talk on the phone to discuss the podcast episodes, record some links if need be and strategise. A brand-new source told me that he had heard Parle had some influence over Scousers involved in criminality in Camping Villamar, on the outskirts of Benidorm, Spain. In 2018 there had been a drugs bust on the huge caravan site and, while Parle had not been arrested, the police did detain three British men, aged thirty-nine, forty-two and sixty-four, and a twenty-nine-year-old British woman, alongside a thirty-six-year-old Lithuanian man.

The Spanish police boasted of the large amount of drugs that had been seized along with a substantial amount of cash and some high-value vehicles: 'The members of this largely British-led organisation thought this campsite, where 2,500 people stay in high season, was the ideal place to base their centre of operations among compatriots. One of the alleged ringleaders of the group resided there permanently and controlled seven plots, with caravans used to store and sell the drugs. Investigators concluded the drug trafficking gang had reached international dimensions and had established a route between the UK and Spain.' The spokesman went on to describe some members of the group as 'quite violent'.

I double-checked my own research with the source. He confirmed his opinion about Parle and Villamar. This caravan site was obviously another place on the Costa Blanca that we should visit. I had a long chat with Mark and he told the BBC that Spain was now firmly on the agenda.

My attitude towards making a trip was, 'Let's book a hotel in Albir and plonk ourselves there for the duration.' As part of working for the BBC, Mark had to complete a risk assessment and advice came back – from far wiser heads than mine – that we should actually use a number of venues and keep on the move. I'd never had to do anything like a risk assessment when working on my previous books, when research led me frequently to Nairn, Scotland, to write about the murder of Alistair Wilson, or travelling alone to socially deprived areas, like Cheetham Hill in Greater Manchester, for *On The Run*. I remember that one cab driver flatly refused to take me to the area. He dropped me on the outskirts, from where I made the remainder of the journey on foot. Just as well I did, because my inquiries led to me being given a scrap of paper with the name of a person who was thought to be responsible for the murder I was researching.

We met with the BBC again in Manchester and then once more made our way to Liverpool, but this time we stayed with friends of Mark a few miles outside the city. That trip was a whirlwind: we got in front of people, tracked down potential witnesses and interviewed people who could make interesting contributions to the pod. We met one guy who really gave us a flavour for the city, particularly with regard to music, and he brilliantly described Liverpool as 'the Nashville of the north'. For the first time in my life I tried mushy peas with my fish and chips. They had been described to me as 'northern caviar'. I'm a convert. I love them. One cab driver

– who, like everyone, got a flyer and was told what I was doing – said he knew Kirk Bradley. He went on to describe him as a man who 'loved the gangster lifestyle'. He told us that Bradley loved guns and he described him as 'bonkers'.

The first three episodes of the podcast were released on 6 February 2020. Two days earlier, Mark, Lewis the producer and I went to a BBC press event where, perched on a high stool, I was interviewed by a host who took questions from the audience of journalists. There were a number of podcasts, but they showed considerable interest in ours, which was very pleasing.

I kept in regular contact with my OSINT guy Kyle who was developing any intelligence we received and I was delighted when he identified a bar in Javea on the Costa Blanca, where it was thought people known to Parle might frequent. By now the Spanish trip was firmly in our sights and we were not going to be short of places to visit. In the meantime, I still had some public speaking events, including visits to schools. I love talking to pupils about my career, crime and criminals, and of course, Kevin Parle. I never accept a fee from schools, I simply ask that they use the money they might have paid me for the benefit of their students or charity.

I was also approached by a young man called Jack Dean, a YouTube sensation, where he goes by the name of JaackMaate. He has more than a million subscribers. He also has an incredibly successful podcast called *Happy Hour* and, when he offered me the opportunity to appear on it, I jumped at the chance. I travelled to north London one afternoon and had an extremely enjoyable time with him and a couple of his colleagues. They all had a sense of humour. They'd never heard stories like mine before. I told them some of the tales from my life working undercover and living in the witness protection programme. The great thing was they were not slow in taking the mickey out of me; I gave them plenty of ammunition. Jack also gave me a fair bit of time to talk seriously about Parle. I was delighted to hear that my interview was one of the most popular podcast episodes Jack had ever put out: many young people got in touch to ask questions about Parle and the hunt for him. I was able to steer them in the direction of our BBC podcast.

I continued to publicise the BBC podcast series wherever I could, across social media and beyond. For me the podcast was no longer ours: it belonged to the public, and they would make of it what they wanted to. Mark had episodes four to six in the can and ready to be released, one each week. From here on in we would be turning the episodes around very quickly, to deliver, as promised, my investigation in as close to real time as we possibly could.

15

HOLA

On Monday 10 February my alarm went off at 2 a.m. I jumped in the shower, fuelled up on nicotine and caffeine and was ready to get going to Spain.

The easyJet flight to Alicante was delayed but the journey to Mark's house, around a largely empty M25, was straightforward. We loaded up and were on our way to Luton airport on a particularly chilly morning. Ever mindful of cash, I had plumped to park in the long-stay carpark where we would catch a bus to take us to the terminal. I saved a whole £17 but came to regret the decision almost immediately, as we stood for what seemed like an eternity in a windy and bitterly cold, pathetic excuse for a bus 'shelter', waiting for the connection.

I don't enjoy flying. I'm not scared of the experience but I just find the hassle of checking in, passport control and security to be so tedious and irritating that I'd rather avoid the whole thing. But it was a necessary evil – realistically, I wasn't going to be able to get to Spain any other way. Once we got airside, we grabbed some food and the oh-so-essential coffee. Mark recorded atmospheric background sound and asked me some questions for the podcast. This trip was planned to give us enough material for a whole episode, although I was quietly confident we would fill two editions with our adventures on foreign soil.

After what seemed like an eternity – a total of three hours' delay – we finally clambered onto our plane. I was not happy with the wait. We settled down into the front-row seats that I'd secured for extra leg-room (extremely important when you're six-foot six-inches tall, like Mark). Despite having consumed around a gallon of coffee that morning, I was asleep before take-off.

The plan had been to head off south to Torrevieja on arrival and immediately check out the Mi Sol holiday park that Parle had reportedly visited back in 2006. The delay meant we needed a rethink. Out of the airport, the ever-affable Mark got behind the wheel of our rather nice hire car, while I handled the satnav (I'd offered to share driving duties, but Mark decided not to spend the extra cash in getting me insured). We headed for Albir. We drove on largely deserted roads while we discussed what to do now. We agreed that we would dump our bags in our hotel rooms, make a couple of phone calls and then head off on foot into Albir.

The primary focus of our interest was the Chillout bar, which Parle had apparently frequented 'quite a lot'. I hadn't been able to find a website for it and the directions I'd sourced were very patchy. I sensed that much of this trip might be about following our noses, going where our instincts told us to go and, in that regard, I trusted Mark implicitly. There had been many occasions in the past few months on which he'd favoured visiting a particular location and speaking to a certain person, while I prioritised something else, and that was fine. After all, we had different driving forces: Mark was making the podcast series, while I was hunting Parle, but these projects were intertwined to the point of being almost

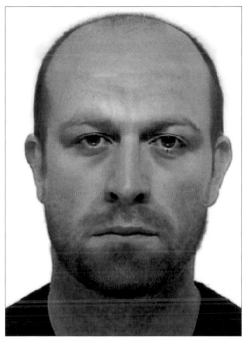

A computer enhanced image of Parle's police mugshot, created by John Moores University. This is a representation of what they think Parle looked like in 2016. ©Shutterstock

A wanted poster generated by the Australian Federal Police, following the reported sighting of Parle in Perth, WA in 2016. ©Shutterstock

Lucy Hargreaves. A man told me, 'Lucy was as beautiful on the inside as she was on the outside.' ©Shutterstock

Liam Kelly. A sixteen-year-old kid. ©Shutterstock

Above and right: I have handed out many hundreds of these flyers in my hunt for Parle. I always carry them. Peter Bleksley

LIAM KELLY
Shot Dead on 19th June 2004

LUCY HARGRAVES
Shot Dead on 3rd August 2005

My name is Peter Bleksley and I believe that those who commit murder should face justice. For over 14 years Kevin Parle has evaded justice. Enough is enough. His time on the run must be brought to an end. If you know anything about the murder of Liam Kelly or Lucy Hargreaves, please get in touch. You can call or text me on 07908 617 694, email me at peterbleksley@msn.com, or submit a report via my website: www.peterbleksley.com.
You can also contact me via social media:

 @peterbleksley   f   Peter Bleksley

I guarantee that I will never disclose your identity.

The smiling Parle. I had this created for for me by a
contact using Face App. Peter Bleksley

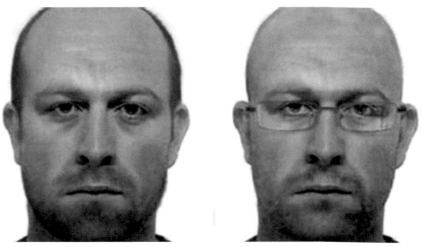

Two more John Moores University computer enhanced pics. Two witnesses have
said the pic on the right, with the glasses, is how he looks now, although he does
not always wear them. ©Shutterstock

Lambourne Road, Liverpool, where Lucy lived
and died. Peter Bleksley

The Chillout Bar in Albir, padlocked, where Parle
was reportedly seen many times. Peter Bleksley

Laying flowers and flyers in Grafton Street, where Liam was killed. This was on the 15th anniversary of his murder, 19th June 2019. Peter Bleksley

Arabic (top) and Thai (bottom) language flyers that I've used in my international hunt for Parle. Peter Bleksley

inseparable. We agreed that we would go wherever either of us wanted to.

From the main road we could clearly see Benidorm and its endless high-rise hotels and apartment blocks. Now, I like a bit of concrete – in fact, I'm a confirmed city boy who could never live in the countryside – but to me, from a distance, it was not the most attractive skyline I've ever seen. Our hotel sat on the outskirts of Albir and suited our needs perfectly. It was spotlessly clean, functional rather than fancy, had loads of car-parking and had a finely stocked bar and very decent coffee. And it was reasonably priced.

The weather was a stark contrast to the early morning chill of Luton airport's long-stay car park. Mark and I now found ourselves getting sweaty as we walked in the warm sunshine of the Costa Blanca towards the centre of Albir. The maps on our phones seemed to have as great a difficulty in finding the Chillout bar as I had had trying to find out anything about it on the internet. We walked for what seemed like an eternity, making one wrong turn after another. I cursed my phone. One upside was that we were getting a good idea of the layout of the town and its main roads. Finally, at a distance of about 150 yards, I could make out the word 'Chillout' on a multicoloured sign. Our pace quickened, but my heart sank when we got nearer the venue I had been so desperate to visit. I could see barrier tape, the kind you might find around a crime scene, stretching back and forth across the patio area at the front of Chillout. This was clearly a no-go area. I crossed the road, muttering expletives to myself. The tape was faded, indicating it had been in position for months. A stout, metal chain was wrapped around the handles on the front door, its ends bound tightly together by a huge padlock.

I must have broken the world record for use of the word 'fucking' the most times in a single sentence as I complained about the time, effort and expense we had gone to in getting ourselves in front of a padlocked door. Once my rant was over, Mark calmly suggested we go to the next-door restaurant to find out what we could. As always with Mark's ideas, it was very smart. We were greeted by a delightful Italian man who proudly showed us around the establishment he had run for the past couple of years. He ushered us to an outside table at the front and, as we sat down, I decided that I needed a beer. Mark fancied one too.

The restaurateur was only too happy to tell us his life story and everything that he knew about Albir. He explained that the Chillout had been run by a Russian woman and had closed for an unknown reason in August 2018, some six months earlier. He had looked into buying the building, thereby more than doubling the size of his fine eatery, but the owners were apparently asking for €300,000, which he felt was way too much. I phoned the source who had steered me in the direction of the venue. She was mortified that it was shut and promised to get back to me sooner rather than later.

A couple of shops away on the other side of the Chillout was another bar. It was quite busy and the best way I can describe it is as being earthy. It wasn't a complete shithole, but you'd probably only go there with your mates rather than with your wife. Mark and I thought it seemed to be a likely place to strike up a conversation about a certain British fugitive. We headed to this new place without much hesitation. Mark and I don't usually have to discuss tactics ahead of our encounters, thanks to the deep bond of trust between us, borne out of the fact that we had quickly learned how the other works and that we had both liked what we'd seen. We'd often just see how events pan out and where they take us.

Sitting outside the bar was a group of English blokes, who were clearly not holidaymakers. Judging by the amount of empty glasses in front of them they all liked a drink. And we all know how alcohol can loosen lips. One of the guys had clearly spent many years doing what they were currently doing – drinking in the sun. His leathery skin was like mahogany and his wrinkles ran deep. His northern accent had a slight slur to it. We sat down alongside the men and I went to get us beers. By the time I returned, Mark had struck up a conversation with these fellas about football, a typical icebreaker of his that I liked.

The football and general chit-chat lasted a full twenty minutes or so before one of them piped up, 'What brings you guys to Albir?' This was going to be make-or-break time. Would we suddenly become so unpopular that we'd have to make a hasty exit, or would the conversation continue? I pulled a bunch of flyers out of my rucksack, handed them around, and delivered my well-practised line. 'I'm an investigative writer, and I'm hunting a fugitive called Kevin Parle.' I had honed my routine.

The atmosphere changed. Not so dramatically that we had to leg it, but the joviality quickly evaporated. Immediately, we were told to be careful, that there was a significant Scouse population in Albir who could be a bit lively and we were strongly advised not to tell people where we were staying.

Albir was situated just five miles from Benidorm and, if you were there on holiday, you might never guess that there is any more to it than it being a pleasant, if ever-so-slightly-run-down town. Now we were scratching beneath the surface and discovering that it had a far more sinister side. We were told that the town was awash with cocaine. Apparently, many of the fifty-to-seventy-year-olds who chose to relocate to the Costa Blanca for a life in the sun were hoovering up industrial quantities of the white stuff, as you might expect younger people to do in the UK. These cokehead cravings had to be satisfied and doing so was lucrative. Criminal gangs were apparently willing to use violence to protect their business interests. One of the guys we were talking to at the bar summed up Albir as 'dangerous'. Happy holidays, everyone.

Back at the bar, our new, leathery-skinned mate, who I will call Virgil, told us how he'd lived in various countries, predominantly Spain, for the last thirty years, six of which had been spent in prison. He didn't want to elaborate on the nature of his crimes, but he did seem to have an in-depth understanding of how the drugs industry worked. If he warned us once to be careful, he had warned us half a dozen times. He was happy to talk to us about crime in the area in general terms, but wouldn't name names, and he didn't know Parle.

I bought the lads a round of the Jägerbombs that they had already been necking at an astonishing rate while – some of them, anyway – managing to remain remarkably sober. This contribution made me very popular and one of the men volunteered that he worked at a nearby bar. During a lull in the proceedings, a couple of the men went to the toilet together, and another went to let his dog out of the car for five minutes. Car? Was he driving his car home at the end of the evening? I feared this might be the case. While everyone was getting on with their own thing and not hanging around to overhear us, the man who worked in the bar around the corner told us to come and see him the following day. We then passed a couple of very informative hours in the company of these men, during which Mark and I turned down numerous offers of drinks (which is very unlike me).

Aside from a snooze on the plane, I'd now been up for some eighteen hours, but I wasn't quite ready to hit my bed just yet. We were only going to have four nights in Spain, and I wanted to wring every possible minute out of our trip. I planned to speak to anyone – anyone at all – who might possibly move my investigation forward. We wandered through the streets in the general direction of our hotel and, as we turned yet another corner, Mark pointed out a very British-looking bar. It had a typical English name, pub sign and frontage. That'll do for me, I thought, and in we strode.

I was very disappointed. Apart from the barman, there was only one customer in there, and we zeroed in on him, sat on a barstool. Oh, well, we were here now, I thought and I ordered a couple of drinks. A gentle conversation went back and forth among the four of us – touching on how quiet business was and the usual bit about football. The barman was all right, as sociable and chatty as someone in his trade should be. The guy on the barstool, in stark contrast, was completely up himself and little time passed before he let us know that he was the owner of the establishment. His favourite – indeed, his only – topic of conversation was himself. I quickly began to zone out of his self-obsessed tedium. It puzzled me that he had such a high opinion about his abilities, because from what I could see he was not exactly the most successful businessman I'd ever met.

After about ten minutes we were asked the inevitable question about why we were in Albir and that prompted me to once again delve deep into my rucksack. The owner took one glance at my flyers before barking, 'Put those away! Don't you dare hand those out to my customers. I know people.' I was tempted to just walk out, I didn't need such nonsense, especially from this twat, but I resisted the urge because I wanted to explore the identities of the 'people' that he knew. He wouldn't give details, attempting instead to intimidate us by lacing his words with a hint of threat. At one point he said, 'Trust me, if I didn't want you to be sitting on that stool, I could make a phone call and you wouldn't be.' I was really tired of him by now and I also didn't want to put any more of my hard-earned cash in his till. Mark, however, being a man possessing more patience – and, on this occasion, showing greater determination – continued to talk in the hope that this man might reveal something of use.

An elderly British couple came in and I chatted with them, keeping half an eye on Mark and the bar owner, just in case things got a bit lively. I did know my buddy was more than capable of handling the situation, as Mark has reported from war zones and other hostile environments; some jumped-up bar owner on the Costa Blanca was hardly the greatest threat Mark had ever faced. He did give it a really good go in attempting to elicit information from the man, but it was not to be.

We reflected on our interesting evening and the area as we strolled back to the hotel. If you are not hunting a fugitive like Kevin Parle, I reckon you could probably have a pleasant family holiday in Albir and remain blissfully ignorant of what lies beneath the sunny façade. But we were on the hunt and delving deeper was what we were here to do.

In my room I set about charging my phones and battery packs, completing my notes, and preparing for the next day. Whilst I hadn't yet received any new and specific information about Parle, I was confident we would. I rested my weary head on my pillow and fell asleep in an instant.

16

POSITIVE SIGHTINGS

I'd love to possess Mark's self-discipline. He would walk ten thousand steps every day, without fail. To ensure that he would hit his target, he got up earlier than me the morning after we arrived, and banked a few thousand yards striding around town.

By way of contrast, I enjoyed a leisurely, continental breakfast, gulped at least three coffees and smoked a couple of fags. If the hotel had served a full English I would undoubtedly have had that too.

We met in the car park at 9 a.m. The Mi Sol holiday park, Torrevieja, was some seventy-five miles away and it would take us about 90 minutes to get there. Fortunately, Mark and I were never short of something to talk about and the journey flew by.

Large electronic gates protected Mi Sol, with a hut that looked like it would house a security guard. I didn't want to take the risk of declaring who we were and being denied entry, so we waited a short while for another vehicle to arrive and the gates to open. Cheekily, we successfully tailgated the next van and drove around for a few minutes to get our bearings. The park was clean and well-kept, housing a mixture of permanent bungalows, small villas and static caravans. Mark parked adjacent to a very pleasant-looking swimming pool that adjoined the bar and restaurant. He prepared his recording gizmo and the microphones while I took some photographs of the pool.

We walked a few paces to the outside area of the bar where some tables and chairs sat empty. A delightful member of staff was rinsing out a mop and greeted us warmly. There was very little need for any small talk, because she was very open and told us she had only lived on the park for a couple of years. No good for us. We were on the hunt for people who had lived on Mi Sol back in 2006, when Parle was reportedly spotted.

We were in for more disappointment when the lady who ran the bar turned up, as she had only been a resident since around 2009. She had heard of Parle, though, and steered us in the direction of long-term residents who had lived on the park for twenty years or more. We did indeed speak with a number of people who had seen Parle on Mi Sol, and who had got to know him to a greater or lesser extent. What follows is an amalgamation of what these different people told us:

'Yes, he was here. Kevin was here for a whole summer back in 2006. A whole summer. He was here with a few of his mates and he had a girlfriend from London.'

'His mates were all Scousers and they could be a bit of a problem. I think the bloke who ran the bar had to ban them at one stage as they were involved in some trouble. They could definitely be violent.'

'I liked Kevin. He was a nice bloke, but he had an edge; he had a side that wasn't so nice. He could be vicious. You couldn't miss him because of his height and his shaven head.

Those leaflets you've been handing out, with the two pictures of him on them; the one on the right, that's how he looked. He had a wispy, ginger beard but that picture is definitely him. You can't mistake him.'

'He used the pool a lot and hung around in the bar. He drank lager, as far as I can remember. He treated the place as if it was his home.'

'Changing money was a bit of an issue for him. He'd be asking people to change a few hundred pounds at a time of English money and they'd change it into Euros.'

'There are a lot of people from Liverpool here and on some of the other sites. He had a proper Scouse accent but it wasn't as strong or as broad as his mates. In fact, I'd go as far to say that he was well-spoken. Big Liverpool fan, I remember that too.'

'At some stage he disappeared. Kevin and his girlfriend went to a villa a few kilometres from here in Quesada. I remember, later that year, Merseyside police sent people down here and interviewed people, took statements and all that stuff. But they were too late. Kevin had flown the nest.'

'Funny thing – well, I suppose you could say it was funny – was that a few years later we were on holiday on the other side of the world practically. We were in Koh Phangan, Thailand. One day I was getting a drink and I saw this man walk past. I said to my friend, "Look who's here." It was him. It was Kevin. By now I knew what he was wanted for so I kept my head down.'

I left Mi Sol with mixed emotions. I was pleased that we had gained an insight into Parle's character. I was also delighted that we had another sighting of him – in Thailand, albeit from around 2008. That witness was unshakeable in insisting they had seen Parle – they knew him so well from the summer he'd spent on Mi Sol. Of course, had this witness done the right thing and reported that Thailand sighting at the time it happened to law enforcement, criminal history may well have been rewritten and my hunt would never have begun. The thought of Parle lording it up around a bar and a swimming pool, a girlfriend on one arm and a pint in the other hand, sunshine on his back, surrounded by his Scouse mates, was very unpalatable. The fact that murder detectives from Merseyside police only turned up after he had left was also a bitter pill to swallow. I couldn't help but wonder if the police had squandered an opportunity to capture Parle on Mi Sol. Yet a spirit of optimism usually courses through my veins and I realised that, once we got this information to the public through the podcast, Mark and I might not be the only people sickened by what we'd heard. These new and previously undisclosed details might encourage people to get in touch with me.

Mark wanted local contributors to paint a wider picture of Torrevieja and we headed down to the popular waterfront. We interviewed a charming man from the tourist board and an estate agent. By now it was mid-afternoon and we were both ravenous. We saw a decent-looking restaurant and both ordered paella, which I love and have enjoyed frequently over the years in Spain. This was an awful example, neither of us finished it, and a couple of hours later Mark had an upset stomach. I'll spare you the gory details. We headed back to Albir, Mark heroically setting his queasiness aside to get behind the steering wheel.

My phone rang en route. It was the Spanish source who had pointed me in the direction of the firmly closed Chillout bar. She had asked her source for clarification about where exactly it was that Parle had been seen, and my source now told me that Parle had been spotted within the past twelve months in a cannabis club on the N332 road, on the outskirts of Albir. Cannabis clubs – or 'cannabis associations', as they are often known – have sprung up in numerous places across Spain in recent years. They operate under strict conditions, with their owners having to first apply for a licence. Drugs most definitely cannot be sold on the premises, but you can go there and smoke your own. I spoke to locals who offered anecdotal evidence to suggest that the police keep a close eye on these clubs and are not slow to close them down if there are breaches. In order to join a club, you have to be a local resident and provide photo ID. The membership fee ranges from about €20 to €100 or more. In return, you can socialise and smoke weed to your heart's content. Smoking cannabis is sometimes also called 'chilling out' and my source thought that this may have accounted for the confusion around the Chillout bar. I was assured again that this cannabis club was definitely where Parle had been seen and I was told that the club was located between a bar called Cocktail and a gym.

On our way back to Albir we stopped in Benidorm and had a meeting with a delightful lady who was the head of British business interests in the region. She gave us a great insight into how the British are viewed in resorts like Benidorm. Apparently, the Spanish love the business they bring, but detest the rowdiness and aggravation. Brits looking for the next, bigger and better high are the main cause of the problems. Occasionally, someone will fall to their death from a balcony or be washed up dead on the beach. These events create local publicity and British newspapers are renowned for sniffing out the most sensational stories to reprint back home. Some UK publications even offer a few quid for a particularly sorry tale. This lady also told us that there are some people, including Brits, who from time to time simply disappear from the Costa Blanca, never to be seen again.

By the time we got back to the hotel it was getting dark. From my room I fired off an email to Kyle, asking him to develop some of the Mi Sol information. I was very interested in trying to identify the girlfriend with Parle in 2006. I really wanted to talk to someone who had been intimate with him, because I thought they might contribute new insights and perspectives on the man. The hotel restaurant was still open and we grabbed a bite to eat. In keeping with the risk assessment recommendations made by the BBC, this was to be our second and final night in our Albir hotel.

The following morning, we made the cannabis club our first port of call after breakfast. It wouldn't be open, but we could scope out the location and carry out a bit of a recce on the neighbourhood, in case we ever wanted to do surveillance ourselves or, more likely, employ others to do so. In a perfect world, where resources were plentiful, I would have sent a small team down there to keep the club under observation for a week, but I didn't have anything like enough in the bank. Mark and I would just have to do the best we could and hope that was good enough.

Thanks to its huge sign, we found the bar called Cocktail easily enough. The gym took a little bit more searching, but the delightful, up-tempo flamenco music that belted out from the venue gave us a bit of a clue. I peeked through the window and saw a group of Lycra-clad ladies performing Zumba or something similar inside. I didn't dwell. There were a few commercial properties between these two businesses and the one we were looking for didn't stand out or seem to advertise itself as what I imagined a cannabis club might look like.

Our target looked like a sleek doctor's surgery or dental practice: white, glass-fronted, spotlessly clean, with a tinting on the glass that I suspected might allow those on the inside to see out. A sheet of white, A4 paper was stuck on the outside of the door, '*Cerrado por reformas*', conveniently translated, 'Closed due to construction work'. There was a mobile number scribbled underneath. I pulled out my phone and had just taken a picture of that piece of paper when a door suddenly opened. Two men were looking at us, both in their thirties I guessed, dark-haired, with southern-Mediterranean complexions.

They confirmed that this was the cannabis club and that it was closed while it was undergoing building work. 'Can we help you?' they asked. Mark already had his microphone at the ready. He had been about to gather my thoughts before the men appeared. I explained that we were looking for a man called Kevin, and one of them said, 'Oh, yeah, tall Kevin, we know him. Why do you want to speak to him?'

At this point I proved to myself that I was too old for this game. In fact, I am cringing with embarrassment as I write this. If anyone was looking for conclusive evidence that I could no longer think on my feet – that I had lost that cutting-edge that kept me alive in the years I spent working undercover – what I did next would demonstrate it. I dived into my heavy and bulging rucksack and produced one of my flyers. I showed the men pictures of Parle that were obviously developed from police mugshots.

The response was immediate. 'Oh, no, that's not Kevin. The Kevin we're talking about is about seventy-five years old. That's definitely not him.' It was clear that these men were not keen to continue the conversation any longer, and Mark and I soon left. We got into the car and I turned the air blue – *very* blue. I could not believe what I had just done.

I told Mark to drive the car to a café across the road from the cannabis club building. I reckoned we could sit outside and have a coffee while keeping an eyeball on the door that the men had opened to us. I was interested to see if there was a sudden rush of activity around these premises. The café was clearly a working-class, local kind of place and Mark and I stuck out like sore thumbs. I didn't see any unusual activity around the cannabis club and after about an hour we left.

Sixty minutes or so had done little to dispel the anger I felt towards myself. After all, what were the chances of a tall, seventy-five-year-old British man called Kevin, living in Albir and frequenting the same cannabis club I'd just visited? Pretty damn slim, I would suggest. What were the chances of the information that I had received from the source being accurate, that Parle had indeed frequented that club and that the people who ran it had lied to us to protect him? A touch more likely, don't you think?

As I said to Mark, when they asked why we wanted to speak to Kevin, I should have just said, 'I've got a hundred thousand euros here for him. Give him a call, get him down here.' That's what I would have done when I was an undercover cop and who knows what might have happened? All right, maybe a tall, seventy-five-year-old British man might have turned up and been confused, but now, thanks to my unforgivable, slack-brained incompetence, we would never know. There was a stronger description I could have used for myself, taking up just one word, but as this particular expletive already features in this book too many times, I will not add to the offensive word count.

Mark – perhaps trying to console me – pointed out that if I had told the men I had a hundred thousand euros in my rucksack, the BBC would have, in all likelihood, taken a very dim view of my deception and I might have put the podcast in jeopardy. I didn't care then and I don't care now. If that had led to a major development in my hunt for Parle I would gladly have sacrificed the podcast. Kevin Parle's capture was far more important.

In a perfect world, with the necessary resources and authorities, the minute we got to the café, I would have deployed a fake phone cell tower (or an 'IMSI-catcher', as they are sometimes known). These devices mimic the operation of a legitimate telecom tower and can hoover up call data from mobile devices within a given area. Keeping with the fantasy, the plentiful surveillance operatives that I would have employed would have kept the cannabis club under observation for a week and would have also had a fake cell tower with them.

There was very little time to dwell on what might have been, which was just as well. My self-loathing could wait. Camping Villamar, on the outskirts of Benidorm, was beckoning. I'd done a bit of research on the site and discovered a story about a Liverpool drug dealer called Scott Hughes, who had gone on the run in 2011 and evaded capture for some five years. He spent some of that time in Villamar.

When he was finally brought before Liverpool Crown Court in 2016, his defence barrister, Richard Orme, told the judge, 'If people think drug dealing inevitably involves a glamorous lifestyle, he has been jet-washing caravans, awnings and patios, as basically the odd-job man at the Villamar camping and caravan site in Benidorm.' Mr Orme said that Hughes spent his time in Spain 'looking over his shoulder' and was 'constantly nervous', fearing that 'the day would come when he would have to face the music'. Hughes apparently met his girlfriend in Villamar, they had two children together and travelled to Dubai. Eventually arrested at Brussels airport, Belgium, Hughes was sentenced to eight-and-a-half years in prison. With his links to Villamar and Dubai, I thought it would be good to find Mr Hughes to see if he fancied a chat. Scott, if you're reading this, get in touch, please.

Villamar had been made famous by the Channel 5 hit show, *Bargain-Loving Brits in the Sun*. The standout star of the TV show was Graham 'Happy Days' Boland, the frequently stressed-out entertainment manager of the site. Having watched the show myself, I was very familiar with Graham and Mark had arranged for us to meet. As soon as we got to the gates and mentioned we were going to meet Happy Days, we were waved through without any further questioning. Graham is box-office around these parts.

The first thing that caught my attention was a large Liverpool Football Club flag, suspended high on a pole that was attached to a static caravan. Row upon row of these caravans, hundreds of them, were positioned on dedicated plots in regimented order. This was a self-contained community, the caravans set inside high fences. It was obviously a popular place to live on a permanent basis, while others enjoyed their summer holidays here and I recognised much of the site from the TV show. Within a couple of minutes, we'd arrived at its heart – consisting of a large bar, terrace and function room. The bar staff were friendly and welcoming; I ordered coffees and a couple of orange juices. I mooched around the bar and noticed signed football shirts on the wall although, as the weather was fabulous, we went outside.

Not many people back home had known about the trip in advance, but one person I did take into my confidence was a freelance journalist. It was no secret that Wayne Rooney's parents had a caravan on Villamar – his was one of the signed shirts inside the bar – and this journalist told me that a tabloid was offering a fair few quid for any information on the Rooneys. I can tell you now that we heard lots of stuff about Wayne's parents while we were in Spain – certainly enough to fill a page or more of a red-top – and the cheque that was on offer would easily have covered all my expenses for this trip with a couple of bob left over. However, I was hunting Kevin Parle, not gathering stories for the press, so whatever I heard was not going any further.

Mark thought that some of the punters in the bar had recognised me and I picked up the way a couple of them looked over and looked away and I heard a few whispered conversations. This wasn't a problem – I wasn't trying to be covert. Graham Boland himself joined us a few minutes later. Over a cup of tea I spent what I can only describe as a joyous hour in the company of Happy Days. He was an absolute delight; as genuine as the day is long, a fabulous raconteur and every inch a thoroughly decent man. I shall not forget our meeting in a long time.

Graham spoke glowingly of Villamar and of the overwhelming majority of people who lived or holidayed there. The Channel 5 show had raised the profile of the camp massively and the benefits for the business had been considerable. Graham, quite rightly, had been given a pay rise and his role was now less stressful. He also has an afternoon radio show called *The Big One with 'Happy Days' Graham* on a local station, Fresh Radio 97FM. Please check it out online, he plays what my kids would describe as some 'banging tunes'.

Graham confirmed the 2018 drugs bust and the arrests. Apparently, those involved had attracted attention by flashing a lot of cash, buying expensive cars, jet skis and speedboats, while having no discernible, legitimate means of income. Some of them apparently had their passports confiscated by police, but were later granted bail. Graham explained that a passport was required for any form of accommodation on the Costa Blanca and some residents had been unhappy about one of the men later returning to the camp without his passport. The law-abiding residents understandably wanted him barred from the site. Some friction was the result of the dispute, by all accounts.

As for Kevin Parle, Happy Days did not know, and had not heard of, my wanted man, yet for all that I could have talked to him for hours: he was such an interesting man with endless entertaining tales to tell, but at last he said his radio show was calling. Later that afternoon, he told his audience about our meeting and the name Kevin Parle got yet another mention on the airwaves. Before he left, he generously agreed to have a photograph with me, which I immediately and rather excitedly uploaded to my family's group chat. One of my sons swiftly and pithily replied, 'At last, a real celebrity.' He was not wrong.

We stayed for another coffee after Graham had left. I had a natter with some of the residents who, like their entertainment manager, were a joy. Many of them were living the expat dream in the sunshine, having purchased their static caravans for up to twenty thousand pounds. They'd made them very comfy, with all the facilities they might need and they knew where to buy the best and most inexpensive meat, fruit and veg. There was great pride in their community and they had been horrified that criminal activity by a tiny minority had caused such a stir.

Mark and I plotted our next move. He reminded me of the rather inebriated man we met on the first night who had told us he worked in a bar in Albir. This contact had invited us to visit him and now seemed like the perfect opportunity as we were just a matter of minutes away. Our man was working in the kitchen and popped out to say 'Hello'. In a quiet moment I asked him if he had anything to tell us about our fugitive but, disappointingly, he didn't. I couldn't help but think we should have probed a bit deeper when he had been under the influence: it might not be a coincidence that he was less forthcoming now he was sober and at work. If he'd never intended to say anything more at the time, why had he been so insistent that we meet him at his workplace?

Despite the lack of new information from our initial target, I made the most of the opportunity of being in a new location: there were a few punters having a bit of lunch and the guv'nor of the bar had no objection to us handing out flyers and explaining what we were doing. A particularly chatty couple of expat Brits steered me towards Albir online discussion forums, as well as a social club and the local bowls club. They suggested we should try yet another bar which they named. My trusted chauffeur in the form of Mark duly drove us there.

We followed the usual drill, getting a drink and sitting at the bar. We engaged with the man who ran the bar, who was very friendly and, as I got into my second Diet Coke, he called over some regular punters and introduced us. I explained my quest and handed a man one of my flyers featuring the computer-enhanced pictures of Parle. I desperately wish I had had a camera focused on this man because his face was an absolute picture. He was transfixed by Parle's image. The only muscles that moved were those in his face as it literally dropped. His bottom jaw moved downwards to leave his mouth slightly open. He was now pale as a ghost. He swallowed hard and looked at me without saying anything. Eventually, he murmured quietly, 'Is he a Scouser?'

I replied firmly, 'Yes.'

He looked at Mark for a few seconds and then back at me. If we had been making a TV documentary this would have been the moment that secured us a BAFTA. He cleared his throat and spoke in a trembling voice. 'I know him. I mean I've seen him, in a bar, here in Albir.'

I honestly thought he might faint and asked if he wanted to sit down. He cleared his throat again, took a deep breath and appeared to be gathering himself. I deliberately didn't ask any more questions, because I wanted him to take the time he needed to recall all that he could. He continued to stare at Parle's picture, puffed his cheeks out and expelled a long breath, repeatedly tapped the picture with his index finger and said, 'It's him, it's definitely him.'

I insisted that he sit down and we got him what looked like it would be a much-needed drink – something soft, as I didn't want alcohol embellishing his recollections. In September 2019 he had been in a bar in Albir – he remembered its name. He saw four people, two men and two women, who looked to him like couples, sitting at a table in a quiet corner of the bar. It was about lunchtime, and he had the impression that these four people had been out on an all-nighter. The woman that he thought was Parle's partner he described as being about thirty to thirty-five years old, a size twelve or, more likely, a size fourteen, with mid-length black hair scraped back into a ponytail. She was of average height, say around five foot four inches. She spoke in a London accent that he described as 'cockney'.

The two women went to the ladies' toilet together, which he thought was strange because there was only one cubicle.

The landlord of the bar apparently saw this as well and, when the two women emerged, the landlord accused them of taking cocaine and told them to leave. One of the women protested her innocence, saying that they had gone into the toilets together to put on lipstick. The landlord was unmoved and insisted that all four leave. My source said that the man he now recognised as Parle stood up and made his way over towards the landlord behind the bar.

Parle was enormous and towered over the landlord, adopting a threatening and aggressive manner, until the woman who may have been his girlfriend forced her way between Parle and the bar and was also facing the landlord. She diffused the situation by persuading Parle to leave and all four did. My source said he got a clear, full-face view of Parle on a number of occasions and he was unmistakably the man in the pictures. He was convinced beyond the shadow of a doubt that the man he saw was Kevin Parle.

The man phoned a friend, another British expat. She joined us a few minutes later. She wanted to hear all about my hunt for Parle and pocketed a few flyers. She listened intently as her friend told her the story he had just told me and Mark. She explained that her own partner had served in the armed forces in a role in which remembering somebody's face was a key skill. If he had seen Parle around Albir he would remember and she promised to show him a flyer as soon as she got home.

I questioned the source at some length to see if there were any other useful snippets I could tease out of him. He maintained that he had told me all he knew and, after exchanging niceties and pledging to keep in touch, Mark and I thanked him and headed straight for the bar where his sighting had taken place. It had since changed hands and nobody knew where to find the now-former landlord. There was no CCTV either; the sighting had taken place five months earlier and the system only stored images for twenty-eight days.

I got in touch with my great friend Julie Clegg, the former police detective and cyber-security expert with whom I'd worked on *Hunted*, and asked her to do some geofencing. This is the examination of all images posted to social media in a particular time-frame and geographical area – in this case, it would be the bar that was the focus of the source's sighting. It was a bit of a long shot – I didn't expect a member of Parle's group to have been stupid enough to upload a photograph to Instagram, but someone else in the bar might have posted a pic at the time and, if they got, say, the back of Parle's head in the background, who knows where that might lead us … ? It was worth a shot.

I wondered about the potential girlfriend of Parle in the bar, the 'cockney'. In my wildest dreams, she was the same person as the 'Londoner' girlfriend from the Mi Sol holiday park in Torrevieja of 2006. It wasn't impossible: the Mi Sol woman had dark hair, as did the woman in Albir. The ages worked too. After we had spoken to the source, I kept asking myself, 'Had Parle really kept the same partner for all these years?' If he had, I thought we were going to be home and dry, because my search would then focus on identifying her. Find her, find Parle. Some days later, someone told me at great length that the Mi Sol girlfriend had since got happily married to someone else and had a couple of kids, so that potential line of enquiry went out of the window. I was still keen to speak to her but could not get access to her. I have not given up on my efforts. Who knows what useful information she may harbour?

Mark and I had originally planned to go on and find some people who had been overheard talking about Parle in a bar further north, in the coastal town of Denia, but we had to consider the importance of that again in the light of this new sighting of Parle. This came alongside our experience with the men from the cannabis club – the 'tall Kevin' conversation – and the reports of drug-dealing in Albir. There could be no doubt that this area would be my primary focus. If we went to Denia we would be declaring our hand and I now wanted to hold that next move back. The Denia witnesses might choose to say nothing to us (in fact, I thought that was probably the most likely scenario), but the point was that they would then know that we knew about them discussing Parle. It might have been a priority to find them when we took off from Luton, but the investigation was taking a different turn and that was just in the nature of this sort of work.

I would have preferred to have stayed in Albir itself for another night, but we needed to follow the BBC's risk-assessment recommendations and move on to a hotel in Javea, some forty miles north. Mark was updating the BBC on a daily basis and they insisted we stuck to the original plan. We had made our presence well and truly known in Albir in the last couple of days and, from a safety point of view, it was probably a wise idea to get out of town for a night, in case certain people came looking for us.

The drive to Javea was a very pleasant one, through typically Spanish towns that were inland and off the more obvious tourist trail. Mark and I had a lot to talk about on the way and after we'd arrived and dumped our bags in our hotel rooms, we drove further on, up to Denia, where we covertly checked out a couple of addresses that might be important in the future. These had been discovered by Kyle in the course of his open-source investigations. We did not knock on any doors. You'll forgive me if I don't disclose too much about that here, because I may well be paying these places and their occupants a visit on my next trip to Spain, whenever that may be. I very much doubt that Parle is still hiding out in these places, but I'm convinced some people there are involved in criminality, that they know Parle or at least know of him and, if they have any sense, they will come to me before I go to them. An investigative writer and his colleague turning up on their doorstep, microphone at the ready, might not be very good for their businesses – legitimate or otherwise. If you're reading this, you know that I know who you are. My contact details are at the back of this book.

Next up from Denia was a former colleague of Mark who lived in a remote village about an hour inland. He still worked in radio journalism and it made sense to make the effort to see him – at least, I enjoyed the views while Mark negotiated some pretty challenging roads. We arrived at a delightful bar and restaurant just as the sun was beginning to set and spent an hour or so in engaging company, which included that of the vivacious and bubby landlady, a lovely northerner. Her bar's walls were adorned with paintings and photographs, and knick-knacks were neatly positioned on shelves and windowsills. Everyone at the table got a flyer, of course, and a brief resume of Parle and the crimes for which he is wanted. I enjoyed a glass of red, while driver Mark had to stick to Diet Coke. Our fabulous host suddenly produced sandwiches and firmly refused any payment. There was never the slightest pause in the conversation and a large part of me wished we had been set to stay there for the night.

I learned that there were stories of crime even in this idyllic, whitewashed, tiny village of narrow streets. Burglary was a problem and the locals were trying to get the police to do something about it. The landlady also told us a funny story about once noticing a small statuette was missing from the ladies' toilet. A young lady had been in the bar that same night and the landlady had not entirely trusted her. It was Mother's Day and the landlady paid a visit to the girl's house and asked her mother what gift she had received. Mum proudly pointed to a familiar statuette. I loved this story and told the landlady I thought she would be a brilliant candidate for the UK police force should she ever want a change of career. She laughed but, sadly, did not seem too keen to follow my suggestion. At least now she knew about Kevin Parle and said she would definitely give me a call if he ever sauntered into her bar.

The drive back to Javea in the dark was a bit of a challenge, but we arrived in time to find ourselves a quite wonderful and reasonably priced restaurant, one of the few that were open on the beachfront in what was the low season. The very welcome and complimentary sandwich had been great, but was never going to be enough to sustain a couple of units the size of me and Mark. We ordered some tapas and a bottle of wine before walking to the terrace so that I could have a smoke. The staff could not have been more accommodating, as they positioned a patio heater above us that meant we did not shiver in the cold night breeze blowing in from the Mediterranean Sea.

My phone rang. It was the man who had seen Parle and his party being thrown out of a bar the previous September. This source had spoken to his friend whose partner used to be in the armed services. Her partner had looked at my flyer and he confirmed that he had seen Parle in Albir – and recently. Unfortunately, this man would not meet us and there were no further details. This was third-hand information and it was far from ideal to leave it at that. I pushed for a meeting, but I was firmly told that was not going to happen. Instead, the source had in mind another bar owner who wanted to meet with me. We arranged a time and location, back in Albir, for the following morning.

Under the warmth of the patio heater, on a deserted terrace, with a glass of wine in one hand and a fag in the other, I told Mark what a wonderful companion, colleague, wise advisor and all round great bloke I thought he was. He ordered another bottle of wine. We had been joined at the hip since the start of this rollercoaster of a project and now we were making progress. We finished the bottle and sauntered back to the hotel. For the avoidance of doubt, we retired to our own rooms.

17

GANGSTER'S PARADISE

I have a pathological hatred of being late. I would far rather be thirty minutes early than thirty seconds late. This stems from my days as a detective when a heavy fine of his own devising would be imposed by my guv'nor on anybody who couldn't get their backside into work on time.

There was nothing more irritating for a police team – who might have got up at 3.30 a.m. for a 5 a.m. briefing – to be held up by the one twat who couldn't wake up on time. The punishment? The wrong-doer usually had to buy breakfast for the entire team or, if the team were too busy to eat, then they would be dispatched to the off-licence to get a bottle of whiskey and beers for the drink at the end of the long day. In all probability the latecomer wouldn't be asked on the next, juicy, early-morning 'spin' – what the police called a search.

You can imagine my horror in Spain, then, when I was awoken not by my alarm, but by my phone. It was Mark and, yes, I had overslept. Obscenities filled the air (mine) as I flew into the shower. When I very sheepishly made my way down to the car park, there was Mark, over-dramatically looking at his watch and me. He had a grin on his face that said, 'You are never going to live this down.' And to this date, I haven't. I only have myself to blame.

We headed to Albir. I'd missed breakfast of course and was absolutely starving but – as part of my punishment – Mark refused to stop until we reached our destination. If I had been in his boots, I would have done exactly the same. Make the miscreant suffer, and quite right too. We returned to the very first bar we had visited, where I ordered the full English. I bought Mark's breakfast as part of my fine.

Sitting where he had been four days earlier was our leathery-skinned, ex-con, expat of thirty years. It was 11 a.m. and he had a glass of beer in front of him – and, judging by the other empties on the table, it wasn't his first. He was very sheepish and a lot less chatty than he had been previously. He couldn't get away from us fast enough: so much so that he left half a glass of beer, something I'm not sure he'd ever done in his life before. Mark and I mused over what had brought about this change in his attitude towards us.

Twenty minutes later, with a clean plate in front of me, I felt human again and it was time to meet our source and his landlord friend. We drove to the appointed rendezvous, where we could be sure that we were not going to be seen or overheard by anyone. On the way I began giving Mark a lesson in counter-surveillance techniques, until he put me firmly in my place by reminding me of the hostile environment training he'd had. Between us we made sure we were not being followed.

My source made all the introductions. We were introduced to the landlord and he did not beat around the bush. 'This town is evil. It is run by criminals. The only bars that survive or thrive are those that allow drug-dealing to take place on the premises or that launder the villain's drugs profits through their tills, or both. You make the business look profitable by buying loads and loads of booze. Some you sell, the rest you give away or throw away, so long as it looks like you are doing a roaring trade, which allows you to put drugs money through the books so it comes out clean the other side. I was approached to launder drugs money and I refused. I don't want anything to do with that shit. I'm an honest man and I don't want to go to prison for these arseholes. Now I can't afford to run my bar. With all the costs, taxes and overheads I have to take a thousand euros a week just to stay afloat and I can't do that. The Spanish have put laws in place to force bar owners to employ locals, which is understandable, but it means you can't pay a young Brit, who might be looking just to fund their time in the sun. People come out here and fall in love with the weather and the lifestyle. They then decide to buy a bar. Only then do they get to know what really goes on. Make sure that you tell anyone who is thinking of doing that, not to. Unless they want their lives run by criminals. I'm selling up and then I'm getting out of here. I strongly suggest you do too.'

I hadn't heard anything that could directly help me in my hunt for Kevin Parle and yet, with his eloquent speech, I couldn't help but like this man. It was sad to see how his Spanish dream had become a nightmare. We nattered for ages about all manner of other things and it was clear how much he yearned for home. We wished him well with whatever he did in the future. We both thanked the source for arranging this meeting and asked him to stay in touch.

Our fourth – and final – night in Spain was to be spent in yet another hotel. Our flight the following day was to leave quite early in the morning and Mark had booked a hotel close to Alicante airport. We arrived in the afternoon and spent time reflecting on what we'd learned in our trip and planning podcast episodes. Mark had some questions that he wanted to record me answering for the show. I also needed to consider if there was anything more that I needed to task Kyle or Julie with. It was now 13 February. The fourth episode of the podcast had been released and I also needed to spend some time on social media advertising it and considering my mainstream media strategy. I now had information that I was sure would interest news outlets.

After suffering the purgatory of flying back to Luton – I won't bore you with the details – I was behind the wheel of my car, driving Mark home. My phone rang straight onto loudspeaker. It was again the source who had seen Parle square up to the landlord of the Albir bar. This time he was short and to the point, 'I've spoken to someone and I can tell you Parle is now in Thailand.' He wouldn't or couldn't elaborate. He didn't want to tell me how he had come across this information. It sounded to me like he just wanted to tell me this snippet and then get off the phone, which essentially is what he did. I tried to contact him many times since but he didn't return my calls or respond to email. Clearly, he didn't want to speak again. I wish he would. I sometimes wonder what prompted his change of heart. Bearing in mind what some people told us about 'evil' and 'dangerous' Albir, maybe I should not be too surprised. I just hope he's OK. He wasn't the only one – some of those who had been in contact from Mi Sol also went completely silent.

18

THE REVIEW

Mark and I were approached by Radio 1 to work on a top-secret project. Only a handful of people at the BBC knew what was going to happen and we were taken into their confidence.

The presenter of the *Radio 1 Breakfast Show*, Greg James, was going be 'kidnapped' at the Brit Awards after party. Over the course of a couple of days, while Greg was held in a secret location, listeners were to be given a series of clues from which they had to try and answer the question, 'Who's Got Greg?'

We began work on this project five days after returning from Spain. Once again we were staying in a hotel, working together on the podcasts we were to release as part of the fun. I was to be based at Radio 1 and would coordinate the hunt for the culprits, as well as trying to identify Greg's location. Mark produced a series of six podcasts over the two days Greg was 'missing'. And fun it was. We worked incredibly hard, as did everyone involved in the venture, getting very little sleep, but we had a blast. Not only did we – and when I say 'we', I mean the wonderful listeners and I – discover that Greg was being held at the top of the Shard in London Bridge, we also found out that the people responsible for snaffling him away were comedian Alan Carr and Radio 1 presenter and singer Mollie King. It was an honour to have been asked to play a small part in such a cleverly thought-out and brilliantly executed bit of fun.

The same day that we found Greg, 20 February 2020, the fifth episode of *Manhunt* was released. Mark and I enjoyed a couple of celebratory glasses with a delightful bunch of talented young people from the BBC and I wound my way home. There was plenty still to do for my hunt for Parle. The podcast had already prompted people to get in touch – and that was great. Law-abiding members of society reported they might have seen him while on their holidays in Spain or Portugal. None of the sightings were recent.

Kyle continued to develop the information we'd gathered in Spain. Our trip had generated enough material for two episodes of the show, but we had to keep looking ahead, not only in investigative terms, but for the rest of the run. I was now sitting on a wealth of intelligence from a wide number of different sources. I couldn't see the woods from the trees. I'd created something that was becoming unwieldy and I was concerned that things might be slipping through the gaps. I knew what I had to do.

Any good detective understands that their work needs to be reviewed, preferably by an outside team which can be completely objective when it carries out its work. My hunt for Kevin Parle was no different, apart from the fact that the only public-facing investigator was me. The time had come to call upon the opinions and expertise of others; to get impartial comment on what I'd done so far that would help me plot the way forward. I did not have a monopoly on good ideas.

Mark agreed that the next episode should consist of this 'review'. My great friend Professor David Wilson was happy to take part, as was Peter Walsh, the esteemed author of *Drug War: The Secret History* and co-author of *Cocky: The Rise and Fall of Curtis Warren*, books which, if you want to know anything about criminals and drugs in the UK, you really need to read. Mark and I had already interviewed Peter for the podcast. He was a mine of information and had decades of experience as an investigative journalist and author.

I decided to hold the review in Liverpool and Mark and Lewis the producer set about arranging a recording studio. David and Peter kindly agreed to travel to meet us and Kyle and Julie Clegg made their contribution via the internet. We began recording the programme with me bringing everybody up to speed with the investigation, including my experiences with Mark in Spain. Clips of our interviews and testimonies from various sources were played into the discussion, among them the conversation with the two men outside the cannabis club. We unanimously agreed about the sudden change of tack with 'tall Kevin': the others were entirely convinced that the man had lied to me when he said that the Kevin he knew was seventy-five years old. They also thought he had realised his mistake of just a few seconds earlier and was trying to protect Parle.

This review drew me to conclude that I needed to focus on Spain, to return and continue my investigations or, in the words of Professor David Wilson, to 'shake the tree', and see what fruit fell off. We said hearty goodbyes before Mark, Lewis and I dashed to BBC Radio Merseyside, where I gave a live interview. Then we hurriedly made our way to the police headquarters in the centre of the city. The DCI greeted us in reception and, as per usual, we had a meeting that was fairly cordial.

Interestingly, the DCI told us that they'd had students from the College of Policing with them that very day, and that they had played sections of the podcast. Apparently, a discussion about the podcast had followed, but we were not told of the content or conclusions. Maybe some enlightened officers were seeing the value of cooperating with such a project? The police did seem to have realised the podcast was a proper, grown-up bit of broadcasting and that I wasn't some fly-by-night self-promoter. Yet our relationship remained very much a one-way street, in that they still wanted me to tell them everything while they told me nothing, or very little, in return. I understood that the police couldn't go breaching confidences, data protection regulations or the Official Secrets Act, but I was only asking simple questions like, 'Was the information helpful?' and a simple 'Yes' or 'No' would help considerably. I'd become increasingly frustrated over the past year.

I left with a handshake from the DCI that bloody well hurt. The pain lingered for a fair few minutes afterwards. He'd pressed his thumb hard into the fleshy bit of my hand between my thumb and my index finger and it felt very strange, not to mention painful. Now, I'm most definitely not a Freemason, but I do know they have various wonky handshakes and my concern was that I'd just received one of them. To this day I couldn't tell you if I had or I hadn't, but I know this, it was not a normal handshake and it was unlike any handshake he had given me in the past.

There should definitely be no room for Freemasons in the police. They say they're not a secret society, but rather a society with secrets. That's bollocks, either way, as far as I'm concerned. They can keep their dressing up, their rituals, their little books, their white gloves and all the other stuff they have. Their loyalty is to each other, rather than to you and me. Think about that: if you're a victim of crime, do you want a police officer dealing with your case who has taken a vow of loyalty to an organisation founded on keeping their own secrets? I certainly don't. I couldn't trust masons to put the victim first, especially if the perpetrator of the crime is also a Freemason. I was delighted to hear recently from a senior police insider that the influence of Freemasonry within the police has massively diminished. I look forward to the day when it has been completely eradicated.

Mark, Lewis and I walked to Lime Street station where we got ourselves some grub. Mark and Lewis were getting a train to London and I was going to Manchester where the media department of Radio 5 Live had arranged for me to appear on *BBC Breakfast*. I was going to sit on the sofa and talk about the podcast. There was a car waiting for me at Manchester station, which was very nice, and the driver, who had driven me before when I'd been on the programme, recognised me and we had a friendly natter on the way to the hotel (that the BBC were paying for, fortunately). I dumped my bags, rang the family, and got my head down nice and early because I had to be up at 5.30 a.m. It was a routine that I'd done a number of times usually to talk about a murder, or a terrorist attack or some other ghastly event.

The next morning the press representative from Radio 5 Live was on hand to greet me. I brought her up to speed with some, but not all, of my investigation. A make-up artist applied some much-needed powder to my ageing and wrinkled face. The interview itself went OK. One of the presenters told me, off-air, that their relative was a police officer who had worked on one of the murder cases. I handed them a flyer – of course. My appearance on the show undoubtedly raised awareness of the podcast and, mission complete, I made my way back to the station.

On the way home, Mark called to say the first six episodes had already been downloaded more than a million times. This was exactly the kind of reach I'd hoped for. Getting a figure for the sheer number of people who now knew about Liam and Lucy and the man wanted for their murders put a huge smile on my face. Mark added that those at the BBC who had commissioned the podcast were also very happy with the numbers.

The next day, 5 March, another edition of the podcast went live, simply entitled 'Spain'. It featured the information that we had obtained about Parle in Mi Sol and elsewhere. The detail we had discovered and the quotes we had elicited from our contributors had never been heard before. The results were astonishing. Information started flooding in from many places and through different means. Some people messaged via my website. Others posted on social media. And the burner phone rang a lot. One source opened with, 'Are you the man who is looking for Kevin Parle?' After exchanging a few conversations with this new contact I felt comfortable enough to give him my personal phone number. A series of lengthy phone calls followed.

This man introduced a completely new thread into my investigation. He said that a notorious Manchester criminal by the name of Michael 'Cazza' Carroll was connected to Kevin Parle via their criminal associate Leon Cullen. Cullen had recently been arrested in Dubai and this source thought that Parle might also be in the United Arab Emirates (UAE).

I researched Leon Cullen and found that his twin brother, Anthony, had been arrested a couple of years earlier in connection with a huge gun and drug-smuggling operation in Warrington. I got an idea of the scale of the operation when I saw that Anthony Cullen had been sentenced to twenty-seven years in jail. Leon went on the run and apparently smuggled himself out of the UK in a specially converted tumble dryer.

His supposed colleague Michael Carroll was also a very interesting character. He had criminal convictions that included one for assault and garnered a lot of publicity, particularly recently, when he was named in the February 2019 trial of men charged with shooting a mother and her son. The court in Manchester was told that Carroll was the alleged leader of a gang called the Anti-A Team. They, apparently, were formed after a fall-out among members of another notorious Manchester gang called, simply, the A Team. A young woman had thrown a drink over someone, a fight followed and feuding escalated into deadly rivalry and eventual bloodshed.

The battle took the life of the A Team's leader, a man called Paul Massey, who was murdered in 2015. The court was told that a revenge shooting that same year targeted a man named Christian Hickey but, according to the prosecution, the hit went wrong and his seven-year-old son, also called Christian, and the boy's mother, Jayne, were instead shot on their doorstep. Both were seriously injured. A very emotive picture of little Christian lying in a hospital bed, bandaged, tubes and monitors attached to him, appeared in the media. Many people were rightfully outraged.

Michael Carroll was young Christian's godfather and had also been the best man at the wedding of his father to Jayne. The court was told that Carroll had contacted the police in 2015, offering information about those he said were responsible for the shooting. He quickly became a target of abuse for talking to the police. Graffiti appeared on the walls of houses in Salford dubbing him 'Cazza grass', 'Coward' and other, very uncomplimentary, things. Carroll eventually fled to Spain.

In February 2016, Spanish police and detectives from Greater Manchester police raided an apartment in Marbella and seized a gun, knives, cash, a knuckle-duster, numerous phones and a weighted body vest. A plot to kidnap, torture and dump Carroll at the bottom of the sea had been thwarted, yet the shootings, stabbings and grenade attacks continued.

A friend of the late Paul Massey, John Kinsella from Liverpool, had been a pall bearer at Massey's funeral and he was shot on 5 May 2018. As he lay on the ground, dying, a man called Paul Fellows stood over his prone body, pointed a barrel close to the back of his head and pulled the trigger twice more. This was an execution – no more, no less. Fellows was arrested and stood trial for the murder of both Massey and Kinsella. He was convicted and, in all likelihood, will never taste freedom again.

When I was told that Parle was connected to Carroll, needless to say I was hugely interested and, over many conversations with the source, during which I earned his trust, I asked him how he had come by this information and where it came from. Was this something he simply thought, or did he know it to be a fact? I knew his information was coming second- or third-hand, but I didn't doubt this informant's intentions to do the right thing in terms of helping me find Parle.

Leon Cullen was arrested in Dubai in February of 2020 and, while he was in jail awaiting extradition, there was a shooting on a road called Monks Place, Warrington, where a man who had apparently been cradling a child in his arms was shot at a number of times. The man was very fortunate to be missed. I was told who that man was. This was an entirely new thread that, potentially, connected Kevin Parle, Michael Carroll, Leon Cullen and Dubai. I decided to reprioritise in order to focus on the development. Mark and I had planned to return to Spain to 'shake the tree', following our case review in Liverpool. This new information changed that. I needed to go to Manchester and Warrington instead. Flights were cancelled and new arrangements hastily made.

Episode eight of our podcast was released on 12 March 2020, the second to feature our findings from Spain, and yet more people contacted me. Bit by bit I was building a more detailed picture of Parle and it appeared the public did not like the man they were hearing of. A steady stream of sentiments along the lines of, 'He must be found' and, 'I hope you get him,' began to be posted on social media and in many other messages.

On 16 March, Mark and I drove to the house occupied by Michael Carroll's in-laws in Crumpsall, Manchester. Only three months earlier, two shots had been fired towards the property, demonstrating vividly that the animosity towards Carroll was not abating. I noticed that their letterbox was firmly bolted. I was not surprised – apparently one of the bullets had been fired at it. I rang the doorbell and a lady came to the front window. She was holding a phone to her ear and indicated that she couldn't talk. I held a business card up to the window and she gestured that I should put it into the post box attached to the wall. I wrote a short note on the back and did exactly that.

We visited a number of other addresses, also without any success. As early evening fell, we drove to our hotel. The global pandemic of 2020 was taking hold and the coronavirus outbreak in the UK made all the headlines. Mark and I plonked ourselves in front of the telly to hear Boris Johnson make a statement. His message was quite simple: if you didn't urgently need to leave your home, you should stay there to avoid getting and spreading the virus. We had a couple of meetings lined up for the following day and we reaffirmed with our appointments that they were still up for it. Whilst both our interviewees wanted to go ahead, the writing was clearly on the wall for further investigation in the field – the countrywide lockdown was just seven days away. I had a number of other addresses in the area that I wanted to visit, but I already knew that to do so would be entirely inappropriate and probably reckless. Mark and I realised that this might be the last time that we spent an evening together for quite some time, so we ordered a bottle of wine.

The following morning we drove to meet a journalist from the *Warrington Guardian*. Adam Everett was everything you'd want a journo to be: inquisitive, enthusiastic, interested, engaging and thoroughly likeable. I told him what I could and vice versa. He appreciated that there were some things I just couldn't tell him, like the identity of my source. He gave us a great insight into the crime and criminals of Warrington. This delightful town of 200,000 people is smack-bang between Liverpool and Manchester and, unfortunately, gets a lot of attention from criminals of both cities. There had been a spate of recent shootings that had blighted the town. Anthony and Leon Cullen were newsworthy in Warrington.

We drove to meet a wonderful farmer who many years ago had encountered Kevin Parle. This hard-working man had been ploughing a field one afternoon when he noticed a Range Rover driving endlessly around his land. As a crop farmer he was not best pleased, hoisted up his tractor's plough and gave chase. At one point he got within about twenty feet of the offending vehicle and jumped out to approach on foot. This was when he saw Kevin Parle, who stuck his head out of the window and gave him a V-sign, before making his escape by crashing through one of his fences. The farmer made his way back to his sheds and noticed shattered pieces of a different fence strewn across his drive. He realised that Parle had reached his farm by driving off a motorway and down a very steep embankment that bordered his land. He rang the police and detectives turned up about an hour later. They showed him a photo of Parle and he immediately identified him as the man who had gestured at him before driving off. It was the detectives who told him he'd just had an encounter with a man wanted for two murders.

The farmer never found out why Parle so recklessly and desperately drove off the motorway and then away from his farm. We speculated for a while; had Parle realised he was being followed? Was he being chased by the police? Did he know there was some junction ahead and did he fear being intercepted? We simply didn't know, but I did wonder, had this been an opportunity to apprehend Parle that the police let slip through their fingers? After being treated to a fabulous sandwich and a bag of crisps by our charming host, Mark and I wished him the fondest of farewells and headed home to prepare for the oncoming lockdown.

Michael Carroll's mother-in-law had picked up my business card and she did call me later. She was an absolute joy. Hard-working, adored her daughter, engaging and chatty. I explained why I wanted to speak to her son-in-law and she vowed to pass on the message. I really wished I could have bugged her phones and other means of communication to be sure of getting his location. I suspected there were a few members of Salford's A Team that would also have liked to have that information. The next day I learned that Carroll was 'not interested' in talking. Michael, if you're reading this,

I still want to talk to you and I will not cease in my efforts to find you. Please expect a knock on the door. I vow not to disclose your address to anyone other than Mark, who will be by my side.

'The Review' episode of the podcast was released on 19 March, and piqued the interest of a number of listeners who got in touch. They'd enjoyed hearing the authoritative voices of David, Peter, Julie and Kyle and wanted to volunteer their own thoughts. One man stridently challenged the view that the men outside the cannabis club had lied to us about 'tall Kevin'. This man was perfectly entitled to express his opinion and the reasoning behind it. I thoroughly enjoy that kind of engagement because it makes me consider alternative possibilities. Please don't ever shy away from contacting me to tell me I'm wrong. (If you can express your views politely that would also be much appreciated.)

We were now at the start of months of UK-wide lockdown, with businesses closed and households confined to quarters. Mark and I were no different. The government regulations instigated to combat the spread of Covid-19 meant we could no longer do face-to-face interviews and like everyone, we faced a few new challenges. Fortunately, witnesses were usually very accommodating as we recorded phone calls with them, usually on the condition that we disguise their voices or hide their identities by using actors. This was particularly important for the two former girlfriends of Parle that I was to speak to.

19

LOCKDOWN

It took a herculean effort to get episode ten ready. Radio studios were closed for all but essential broadcasting and Sunetra Sarker had to record her narration links at home and email them to producer Lewis. He was marooned in Spain for a while but, somehow, managed to get back to the UK just in time to put the show together. Other voiceover actors recorded their contributions on their smartphones. It was far from ideal, but the whole country was facing similar issues under lockdown. Everyone simply had to go the extra mile, and they did — such was the goodwill that Mark and the podcast had created. It was a minor miracle that we were able to finish the show.

We had one more part of this latest episode to finalise, on the advice of the BBC lawyers, who said that we needed to make a few tweaks. They had been brilliant, courageous and enormously supportive throughout and helped us to avoid creating an opportunity for anyone wholly undeserving to sue us. The lawyers suggested we could say Michael Carroll was believed to be 'connected' to Kevin Parle but no more. The informant had told me that Carroll's involvement went deeper, but I had not been able to obtain any supporting evidence and that meant the information had to be treated with great caution. People could have any number of motives for contacting me, as I had learned to my cost via the source who had claimed to see Parle walk his child to school in Liverpool.

I was already hyper-vigilant around Carroll, in case this new source was one of his enemies, seeking to use me as a vehicle to spread untruths. That was one of the reasons why I had done all I could to speak to Carroll himself. Naturally, I would have questioned him about any involvement he might have had with Parle.

I also sent an advance copy of the episode to the DCI in case the police wanted to speak to me about Carroll, Leon Cullen and the Dubai connection. They didn't then and have never asked me anything about that line of enquiry. Have they investigated it and found it to be untrue? I don't know, unfortunately. Are they currently investigating it further? I refer you to my previous answer. I also sent an advance copy to Adam at the *Warrington Guardian*, as per our agreement, giving him the chance to get an article ready to go as soon as the episode landed the next day. By about 8.30 p.m. that night I had everything done and dusted. I couldn't decide whether to wait until just after midnight, when the episode was due to go live on the BBC app and website or whether I should just go to bed. I was hopeful that the new information would motivate people to contact me in the way that previous episodes had. There would have been even more to reveal if our trip to the north-west hadn't been cut short by the wretched virus, but I felt episode ten was very strong. I went to bed feeling confident that more information was going to come my way.

I was convinced that hearing fresh, original detail helped the audience to understand that I was out there and pushing the hunt for real – working on the ground, going wherever I needed to, meeting and listening to people, knocking on doors, shoving flyers through letterboxes, engaging with the media and going to great lengths to preserve the identity of sensitive sources. Throughout the series we had disguised witnesses and I trusted that all these factors taken together would give people greater confidence to message me via text, Facebook, Instagram, WhatsApp, Twitter and my website. Then there was the burner phone – so many people have contacted me on that number: it was the best ten quid I ever spent.

It was no surprise that I woke up at 5.30 a.m. I flew out of bed, dashed downstairs, put the kettle on, fired up the laptop and iPad, checked the burner phone and my personal phone. The episode had landed without any issues. I got myself ready for the day and plonked myself upstairs in the office, in front of the laptop. I was delighted to see that the *Warrington Guardian* article had been posted and it was good. I had been impressed by Adam when we first met him the previous week. My admiration was only enhanced by the quality of his article. I completely understood why his piece majored on the Leon Cullen aspect, because the Cullen twins, as Warrington men, remain such a big story for his newspaper. But he painted the full picture – Parle and Carroll got a mention, as did the podcast. I was more than happy.

It was time to get on social media. As a result of reports of sightings of Parle in Thailand and the references to Dubai, I'd had my flyers translated into Thai and Arabic. I posted those as far and wide as I could, as well as announcing the arrival of the latest episode and uploading an image of Michael Carroll. I had quite a bit to do online.

I'm a huge fan of Twitter. I think it's a fantastic way of reaching people and, of course, promoting things. I also have a lot of fun posting my dubious attempts at humour. It is far and away my favourite social media platform and my 24,000 followers are a decent audience for a Z-list personality like me.

Facebook's all right – I've been on it for years and it can be very helpful; I have set up groups or pages that draw in people and they do spend time poring over my material. My page concerning the unsolved murder of Alistair Wilson is still up and running. People continue to engage with it and, who knows, maybe one day somebody will contact me via that page and tell me who killed Alistair.

However, I really don't like LinkedIn. I think it's where people with letters after their names go to spout off about how bloody brilliant they are and how bloody brilliant everybody else should think they are. I find it tiresome, boring and tedious and I very rarely encounter real engagement there. I still suffer it, only because it's there and I think I should use it, but it is far from my social media platform of choice.

On the day of the latest episode release, it took me a couple of hours to make all the postings. I then sat and waited, which I'm not brilliant at because I'm an impatient sort; I want things *now*. I've always been like that, ever since I was a kid. By the time lunchtime came around we were really up and running. The burner started to ring. Messages came in from Instagram and my website. Episode ten had clearly had the effect I'd wanted.

I'd always wanted to get an insight into the psyche of Parle from a former girlfriend and now I was about to get not just one but two (just like buses …). Both of those who now stepped forward were, understandably, only willing to talk if they had their contributions anonymised. I gave them my word and both women went on to explain how controlling Parle was.

One said, 'He was confident and chatty when I first met him. He was very at ease around women, but I soon learned to my cost that he was violent and manipulative. On the outside he was charming, polite, engaging; a charmer who wanted to impress. But when it was just the two of us that could change in a flash. He could be nasty. But as far as his friends were concerned, he was a big character, no more than that. I don't know if they simply didn't pick up on his menacing ways, or they did and they ignored it, or used it to their own ends. I've read books about domestic abuse since I was with him and he fitted the bill as an abuser because of his threatening ways.

'I kidded myself he cared about me, but he was simply controlling me. He'd open the door for me if we went out, flashed the cash a bit – old-fashioned courtesy. He played at being the alpha male, a gentleman, and he loved it. You could tell he went to a good school; he could handle himself in a restaurant. He was articulate, clever and his manners were good. He could talk about many things, including opera. There was no shortage of cash, but I wouldn't say he threw it around. He'd pay for meals but didn't spend that much on drink. I rarely saw him drunk. He definitely wanted to do something that earned him a lot of money.

'But I knew he could turn. He was jealous and possessive – who was I talking to? Who had I seen? Why hadn't I picked up the phone? If I had something else on and he decided he wanted to see me, he would tell me he'd threaten the people I was going to see to make sure that I went out with him. He had this thing about his family not really loving him, but I don't know if that was true.

'His driving scared me – he was aggressive and nasty and drove way too fast. He was regularly violent to me and I lived in fear of him.'

The other woman, equally courageous in committing her experience to tape, echoed much of what you've just read. She added a story about Parle showing her a video on his phone of his dog chasing and disembowelling sheep in a field. Parle apparently thought this was hilarious. She did not.

The testimonies of these sources would both be going into the next episode. Once again, I called upon a favour from my great friend David Wilson. The country's leading criminologist listened to them and had this to say about Parle: 'It seems to me that both girls are telling the same story. The man that they meet presents as one thing in public but is another personality entirely when he's in private. He's charming and they're not necessarily, it seems to me, put off by his bad-boy persona or by his reputation. I didn't get the impression that these women were naïve; they're fascinated by him and he understands that too.

'And I suppose what I'm picking up is that they're both describing a classic "psychopathic personality". Now, I hate it when people use that label because there's so much bunk written about psychopathy that people think they know what it's all about and usually they don't. And for me, I think of it – or try to explain it – as a personality disorder which has three very different layers. Firstly, the person that's the psychopath has an arrogant, deceitful interpersonal style, which will involve him being deceitful, glib and grandiose. And if you think about some of the things that the women say, you can pick up on that grandiosity. Parle's knowledge of opera, for example, sprung out at me when I heard the girlfriend speak. He went to a good school. There's lots of money; he flashes the cash – there's that glib and grandiose interpersonal style. Secondly, the psychopath has a very defective emotional experience which means that they show very little, if any, remorse. They won't take responsibility for what they've done. They have poor empathy. And in relation to what those two women said, with Parle you get the sense that he doesn't actually understand the impression that he's creating on them, because he's so wrapped up in himself. He doesn't care about the impression that he's making on them. Then, the third layer would be behavioural manifestations of irresponsibility, impulsiveness and constantly sensation-seeking. Again, what stood out from what these women said was, for example, driving his car too fast. That's very typical of irresponsibility that the psychopath would show.

'But I think, again, you've got to remember that, initially at least, psychopaths are fun to be around. They say and do things that you or I would never dream of doing and it's only very gradually you realise that they're dangerous. Of course, by then, when you realise that they're dangerous, that the private reality is different to the public impression, you've already allowed them to get close. And that closeness is used by them to manipulate you.'

Knowing what we now do about Parle, who on earth would want to harbour and hide such a man?

20

LET'S TALK ABOUT SEX, BABY

It was 29 March 2020 and the coronavirus pandemic completely dominated the news agenda. Millions of people faced extremely worrying times across so many aspects of their lives.

I thanked my lucky stars that I was confined to my office with a considerable amount of information to research, two more podcast episodes to work on and this book to write. I had rarely been busier. I'm at the age at which many of my peers are living in the sun, playing golf, bouncing grandchildren on their knee – or maybe all of those things, but not working. I simply cannot comprehend not working. I have an energy and enthusiasm for work that I had when I was half my current age. I fully appreciate my work is not physical, and that I'm doing what I want to do and for that I am extremely grateful.

My motivation to keep going now stems from the time, long ago, when my police career was cut short following the catastrophic two-year spell I spent in the witness protection programme and my subsequent breakdown. I was medically retired from the force after twenty-one years. I'm convinced that there is a residual frustration that gnaws away at me, deep inside, because I did not see out my full thirty years of service. I feel like I still owe the public a debt. I guess I remain a detective and I just can't shrug that off. In my head I'm still a public servant. Perhaps that is why I do what I do.

Among the many people coming forward in my hunt for Parle now there was a woman who clearly had some considerable insight into the sex industry. Not for the first time, I was convinced I was in touch with a person who knew more than they were telling me. I had to park those feelings and just be grateful for any information I got. She told me about the sex industry in Benidorm and other locations on the Costa Blanca. I beat myself up a bit when I thought of Parle because this was an area that I hadn't considered before and most definitely should have, bearing in mind what I was repeatedly hearing about him. He was alleged to have connections to organised crime, to have spent time on the Costa Blanca, and was a philanderer and clearly had a strong libido that needed satisfying. It would have made sense to look into whether he utilised sex workers somewhere along the line.

Put yourself in Parle's position: if you have a physical need that has to be satisfied and you're a fugitive on the run, you might not hang around in bars, restaurants and nightclubs trying to meet someone. It may be easier, safer, and more convenient to use a sex worker who provides a service, takes payment in cash and disappears into the night, keeping the details of their client entirely secret. I now knew that Parle did have girlfriends while he'd been on the run, but this sex-worker thread really seemed worth exploring.

My contact told me that sex workers were not going about their business as they once had. She told me that many of them had now returned to their home countries. Bearing in mind Parle's aggressive and potentially violent nature, she directed me to consider the prospect that he might have pissed off a sex worker or two in the past. She sent me details of websites that I might want to reach out to. This work is very much ongoing.

Another contact explained the intricacies of dating apps such as Tinder. Her in-depth knowledge stemmed from an experience she'd had with an unfaithful boyfriend who had apparently travelled a lot with his work. He had used these kind of apps to arrange clandestine and short-term sexual encounters wherever in the world he found himself. She explained how he created false profiles and suggested I might try the same, as some kind of honey trap. I was very interested in what she had to say, but had doubts about this sort of tactic. Firstly, I thought it unlikely that Parle would himself use an app. Posting a photograph of himself would be ludicrously foolish for a man on the run. He was too smart to do that. Secondly, I didn't want to ask someone to create a false profile on my behalf: I felt that would leave me open to criticism.

I did use my existing profile page on the Facebook app to distribute Parle flyers around the world. I get friend requests all the time, many clearly from spammers, but some who seem halfway legitimate and many of these come from Thailand. Some are women who seem to be looking for a sugar daddy in the UK or something like that – who knows? – but I usually accept their friend requests and, if they start a conversation with me on the messaging service, I quickly attach a copy of my Thai-language flyer. Some ask about the reward and I ask them to circulate the flyer to all their contacts. As far as I'm concerned this is all fair game in my hunt for Parle.

Many years ago, a friend of mine married a Thai chef who was working in the UK. The chef and I became great friends and, even though the couple have since divorced and he's returned to Thailand, we have remained good muckers. He's completely on board with my hunt and has links to Koh Phangan and Pattaya, places where Parle has reportedly been seen and my mate is really putting himself out, trying to spread the word. He tells me that someone who lives in a tiny, off-the-beaten-track village in Thailand could have their life changed forever if they were to receive the twenty-thousand-pound reward. That work is ongoing.

Dubai was another story. I was really struggling to get a knowledgeable contact or reliable source there. I visited the city about ten years ago, when I was bodyguarding a very young boy whose billionaire father had disappeared – the father was later found to have been murdered. This child's mother had access to quite a bit of money and she did like a holiday. I didn't see much of the emirate when the family went there. I occasionally got to lie on the beach and do a bit of sunbathing, but I didn't get into the heart of the city or get to understand the culture of the place because we rarely ventured out of the very expensive hotel complex. I didn't complain because the pay was good and the sun shone. We kept the kid very safe indeed.

At last, by luck, I was contacted by a journalist with links to Dubai. He was researching a story from way back in the 1980s that I had some involvement in and we got nattering. I got a hugely interesting insight into Dubai. Essentially, the only news stories that get into its media are government-sanctioned. I was told that if I harboured any hopes of getting publicity for my hunt for Parle, I should forget them right now.

I naïvely asked this journo if there was a sex industry in Dubai. He said, 'It's prevalent, it's popular and it's a big thing.'

I thought I'd been clever getting my flyer translated into Arabic. This journo put me in my place by telling me that the languages spoken by the people in Dubai who I really should be reaching – the maids, the cleaners, the drivers and the gofers – were mainly Urdu and Tagalog, a Philippine language. He told me those people are far more likely to come into contact with a fugitive than those who occupy the higher echelons of Dubai society: Arabic speakers would not need to lower themselves by hanging around with Scouse or Mancunian scallywags.

I took some time out of my work to lighten up with a bit of fun on Twitter. There was no harm in trying to raise the mood when the news channels were so gloomy, as they were at the height of the coronavirus pandemic. I posted that today was 'national "I've put on a stone already" day'. I knew that I'd eaten enough chocolate biscuits and done so little exercise in the previous couple of weeks that my jeans were a bit tighter than before lockdown. I posted a short video of me playing Subbuteo, an old-school football game that I played endlessly on my carpet with my mates when I was a kid. This clip showed me scoring a goal for QPR (of course) and celebrating wildly.

Somebody tweeted back about the podcast. They asked, 'What's happening? How many episodes are left? How long's it going to run for?' They were also very complimentary about it. Chancing my arm, as I have done all my life, I retweeted their lovely comments and their question about how long was it was going to last and into that retweet I copied in the head of the BBC Sounds app – the man who originally commissioned the podcast. My own reply was, 'I don't know what's going to happen. There are two episodes left. Whether it gets another series or is extended is way above my pay grade. I frankly don't know.' Within a matter of seconds the head of BBC Sounds responded, 'Extended. Keep looking.'

I was thrilled. I got on the phone to Mark, because it would be his job to negotiate the length of the extension. At least I now knew that episodes eleven and twelve would not be the last. There would be a few more quid to keep us going and although we couldn't fly or get a train anywhere during lockdown, it was great to have this support from the BBC. This was cause for minor celebration. I emailed Lewis the producer and narrator Sunetra with the news. I celebrated this extension by having dinner with my long-suffering family, who have to put up with a lot from me, and by opening a bottle of red.

Not every day was filled with such positive news. Like most jobs, hunting a fugitive comes not only with productive times but also moments of frustration. I'd spent a considerable amount of time trying to develop a source who lived permanently in Dubai, without any success. Living under a regime headed by Sheikh Mohammed bin Rashid Al Maktoum would not be my own choice, but I can understand why many people may choose to live there, with a sunny climate and a well-paid job. Personally, I'd far rather live in a flagship democracy like the UK, enjoying our diverse and independent media and having the freedom to pretty much say and write what I like.

Nevertheless, I was given the contact details of a couple of Brits who had lived in Dubai for many years, but they were very reluctant to speak to me. To be more accurate, they bottled it. I had heard tales and wanted to know more about 'Dubai brunch', which apparently occurs on a Friday or Saturday – well-heeled expats from Britain and elsewhere go to swanky hotels, stuff themselves full of delightful food, and basically get on the lash. Of course, Parle, if he has ever been to Dubai, would surely be very foolish to go to such a jolly, for fear of standing out from the crowd and being recognised.

As the state broadcaster only told good news, I was not surprised to discover that the media had never given any coverage to the arrest of Leon Cullen and his subsequent imprisonment, awaiting possible extradition. Likewise, I could find no trace in the Dubai media of the arrest of Lee Eedle, another Liverpool man who was detained in December 2015. Apparently, he was subsequently later bailed, but I cannot find any confirmation of this.

Undeterred, I decided to approach a couple of newspapers that I thought might be persuaded to grant me a column inch or two – or, at least, have a chat off the record. They didn't have an email address, but I did find their telephone numbers. I rang those repeatedly all day, with no answer whatsoever. Maybe their staffing had been stripped to the bone because of the virus and lockdown, but I was getting more and more frustrated with each unanswered call.

My day was interrupted when I had to do a couple of UK radio interviews. I was asked to say whether or not I thought the UK was turning into a police state because some jumped-up lord had suggested that it was. I didn't mince my words in saying what a complete load of nonsense he'd been spewing. The sense of injustice stayed with me for some time and I ended up getting up early one morning and writing an open letter to the nation's police officers which I posted to social media. It really took off and ended up having more than five thousand 'likes' – the most any tweet of mine has attracted. Over the next couple of days, I gained hundreds of new followers – who were, of course, treated to tweets about Parle and my hunt.

There was one bit of bright news. I'd applied to join the International Police Association (IPA), which has 360,000 members worldwide, and I heard that my application had been approved. The man who'd suggested I join was a serving police officer nearing retirement and he was really excited by my hunt. He saw my approach as forming some sort of a template to follow when he leaves the cops himself because he'd also like to hunt fugitives. He told me there are thousands of them that need catching. Fair play to him, he seemed like a top bloke. The big question was how he'd get paid for that kind of work – essentially, he'd be a private citizen doing the police's work for them and I don't know where he'd get funding. Maybe he'll also get a book deal and a BBC podcast! I wished him all the best and he arranged for the IPA to interview me for their magazine. My frustration returned when he told me the IPA insisted on interviewing face-to-face and, of course, no one knew when the virus would retreat long enough to do that.

With the latest episode of the podcast available, I was hoping that renewed activity and the mention of Michael Carroll might interest the *Manchester Evening News* and other local media outlets who had already written and broadcasted numerous stories. Unfortunately, I didn't hear a peep from them and decided instead to spend a hundred pounds to promote a tweet featuring Michael Carroll's picture. A promoted tweet gets featured more prominently in the Twitter feeds of a selected audience and, while it felt like a lot of money for a few words, that tweet ended up having 49,000 impressions (or views) and I didn't think it was mere coincidence when some new sources reached out to me.

I was told a very interesting tale by a man who was convinced he met Parle in Thailand, about ten years or so earlier. The interaction had begun in a very cordial way, mostly discussing football, and the pair had shared some chips. For no discernible reason, Parle had allegedly suddenly become very aggressive and would have flattened this man if they'd been in the UK. My source became very concerned for his safety and beat a hasty retreat.

I continued to investigate the Thailand connection. A contact in the country sent me the details of Facebook groups in Pattaya and Koh Phangan, some of which were run for and by expats. I had to wait a few days for my membership to be approved and I then sent them my history with Parle to date, together with the details of the podcast and I uploaded English and Thai versions of the flyer. One group were particularly interested to hear more details. I was happy to oblige. But my efforts to engage with groups that represent sex workers drew a blank. I was not surprised – the most basic of internet searches on my name would show that I was a former cop and that would explain the reluctance of related organisations to engage with me.

I also reached out to police Facebook groups, one of which was for retired Met police officers while another was for officers who had served in south London. A number of ex-cops in this second group knew me. I thoroughly enjoyed spending an hour or two hooking up with old names from the past, but my motivation was mainly spreading the word about Kevin Parle. Some of the group members were living abroad and I posted all versions of the flyers on the group's page and asked members to circulate them far and wide. There were some very positive responses.

As with my Thailand research, I vowed to keep digging.

21

REASONS TO BE CHEERFUL

Mark and I had long wanted to speak to the National Crime Agency (NCA). After all, Parle featured on their most-wanted list and I was keen to ask what resources, if any, were being applied to the hunt.

I didn't expect to get a reply, being convinced they would adopt a similar attitude to that of Merseyside police – in other words, share bugger all with me – but there would be no harm in asking. Mark hoped they might like to speak to us about Operation Captura, a hugely successful venture to find and detain British fugitives living abroad, particularly in Spain.

Operation Captura had been launched in a blaze of publicity in 2006. There was no doubt that it had been a resounding success. By February 2020, only a dozen of the ninety or so fugitives targeted by the NCA remain at large. That dirty dozen includes Kevin Parle. Periodically, the NCA have launched fresh press appeals for Captura and they always seem to garner plenty of media coverage. They work alongside Crimestoppers, an organisation that promises complete anonymity for anyone who wants to provide information. They have shown innovation – on at least one occasion they have hired a flatbed truck with a huge electronic screen and driven around the streets of the Costas in Spain, flashing images and details of wanted fugitives.

There have been many notable individual successes with Captura: Matthew Sammon was arrested in 2016 at a fairground site in Fuengirola less than twenty-four hours after an appeal for information on him. He was wanted for possessing and distributing indecent images of children. William Paterson was arrested in Madrid in 2014 in connection with the murder of a man named Kevin Carroll in Glasgow, some four years earlier. There have been dozens of others. Christopher Guest More Jr for one – he was in the NCA's sights and was eventually charged with murder and a number of other offences dating back to 2003 at a farm in Tabley, Cheshire, where a man called Brian Waters was tied to a chair, whipped, burned and assaulted with a staple gun.

Waters was hung upside down and then beaten and sexually assaulted with an iron bar. He suffered no less than 123 injuries which proved fatal. Waters' two children, who were young adults at the time, were forced to watch much of this dreadful attack on their father. Three men were arrested and were later convicted of Mr Waters' murder. James Raven, Otis Matthews and John Wilson were all given life sentences. Christopher Guest More Jr went on the run and evaded capture for sixteen years. In 2019 he was arrested in Malta. The NCA were understandably delighted. A spokesman said, 'The NCA has supported Cheshire constabulary with their investigation, using some of our specialist capabilities and our international network of officers, in his pursuit. We have waited a long, long time for this moment. We were never going to give up in the hunt. Other fugitives should really look at this and remember how tenacious UK law enforcement is.'

An assistant chief constable from Cheshire also weighed in. He said: 'Our determination to find Christopher Guest More Jr has not faltered and, over the years, we have remained committed to locating him. This latest development highlights the close working relationship between Cheshire constabulary and the NCA, along with law enforcement agencies abroad, and I would like to thank colleagues for all of their assistance.'

In 2018 a notorious fugitive called Jamie Acourt was arrested in Barcelona, also as a result of Operation Captura. He had come to prominence many years earlier as a suspect in the racist murder of Stephen Lawrence in Eltham, south London, although he was never convicted of that crime and has always denied any involvement. Acourt had been on the run since 2016, wanted by the Met in connection with drug offences. After his capture a senior Spanish police source told the BBC that Acourt had taken 'great care' and deployed 'plenty of security measures' to avoid getting caught. 'He had protection. He had help. He didn't live a normal, relaxing life. He was using false identities, false names.'

The NCA used Acourt's arrest as an opportunity to publicise their work, as they should do, and a spokesman told BBC Radio 4's *Today* programme that many fugitives 'believe they can hide in plain sight', among Spain's large British expat community.

Mark and I had first reached out to the NCA not long after we began work on the podcast series. They refused point-blank to speak to us. Mark had the same response now, as we were approaching the end of the first series. The question was, why didn't they want to be interviewed? Was their failure to catch Parle after more than fifteen years such an embarrassment? And did that mean they were afraid of the questions which

Mark and I might put to them? I had made it perfectly clear to the Merseyside DCI at the very start of my hunt for Parle that I was not setting out to cause anyone humiliation and that remained the case. If my fugitive was captured as a result of information I received it would surely look good for the NCA if they could say that they had cooperated.

That was the case for Merseyside police. They could always say that we have enjoyed what their DCI has described as an 'informal' relationship. Feel free to interpret that however you want – I'm still not sure what it means. I will never forget the DI meeting us for the first time, alongside his DCI, leaning forward and saying firmly, 'We will not be embarrassed.' Again, feel free to make of that what you will; I've spent a disproportionate amount of time trying to figure out the subtext, if indeed there was any. To this day I just don't know. But I can say that I haven't had any kind of dialogue at all, however distanced, with the NCA.

I had a lengthy conversation with a retired British police officer who had worked for the NCA in Spain. I got a great insight into how the Spanish national police and the Guardia Civil operate, where they're in competition with each other and where they cooperate. The arrangement sounded strikingly familiar to the way in which British law enforcement agencies work, which publicly is all sweetness and light while, in reality, personality clashes and opposing goals sometimes cause conflict. The national police and the Guardia Civil do agree in taking a very dim view of British villains who base themselves in Spain, whether they be on the run or actively carrying out criminal activity. They love the publicity that they get when such criminals are captured. This may go a long way towards explaining the huge successes of Operation Captura.

Many years ago, my drugs squad at Scotland Yard would frequently clash with what was then HM Customs and Excise. They would be keen to arrest a courier, inevitably a small player in any criminal organisation, at an airport with a large quantity of drugs, whereas we would want them to be allowed through so that we could follow the consignment and catch the bigger players, albeit at the risk of seizing a smaller amount. Sadly, different law enforcement agencies will often clash. When they do, in my experience, the only people that benefit are the bad guys.

Both Merseyside police and the NCA have been very quiet about their hunt for Parle since my quest began. Aside from a brief appearance on *Crimewatch Roadshow* made by an NCA officer who mentioned Parle, very little has made the news other than press releases from them, and again, I wondered why. The NCA's refusal to meet Mark and me smacked of an unwillingness to be scrutinised. I hoped that in the not too distant future they have similar things to say about a six-foot six-inch, broadly built Scouser as they did about More Jr and Acourt.

At the trial of the men convicted of killing Brian Waters, the court was told that the attack on him revolved around a dispute over drugs and cash. This brings me to another point, not directly connected to Parle, but something very important that needs stating all the same. It's this: I have lost count over the years of the number of murders that I have researched, written about or commentated on that have come about as the result of drugs. The majority of my policing career was spent investigating international drug importations and countrywide distribution networks. And there is only one conclusion I can draw. Our prisons are bursting at the seams because of the drug trade. Being sent to jail is clearly not a sufficient deterrent to people who want to import and deal drugs for a living. The Misuse of Drugs Act 1971 is still in force. Repeated governments have followed a prohibitionist stance on drugs for fifty years yet more people are taking drugs now than ever before. The increasing demand for drugs simply will not go away and there are many people willing to break the law in an effort to satisfy that demand.

The illegal drugs industry is absolutely enormous. It is worth billions, if not trillions of pounds, dollars, euros and so on every year. And yet we leave the entire industry in the hands of crooks. There can be no regulation in illegal activity and disputes can only be settled one way – with violence. Drug dealers do not have their customer's best interests at heart. They merely want to sell more drugs and, often, tempt them onto more addictive substances. The drugs they sell are not made under licence, nor are they subjected to any form of regulation. Some of the substances within these drugs are highly toxic and consequently very harmful. Drug deaths are on the rise.

I fully appreciate that millions of people take drugs recreationally while spending the rest of their time holding down responsible jobs and providing for their families. They have a good time when they're taking drugs and they do not commit crime to fund their drug-taking. This group of users far outnumber the hapless, problematic addicts. Under our current prohibitionist regime, untold lives are lost and billions of pounds of taxpayers' money is, quite simply, wasted. Talking of waste, for all the people me and my colleagues have sent to jail, and for all the years I have spent pretending to be a gangster, are there less drugs and guns on the street nowadays? Of course not. That is why I look back on so much of my police career and think that it was a complete waste of time. People still choose drug-dealing as a lifestyle when in all probability, that choice will end in either imprisonment or death – or both. It is time for a radical rethink.

The illegal drugs industry must be wrestled from the vice-like grip of organised crime. That will only come by legalising and regulating all drugs. I'm not suggesting that this will be easy, for organised crime will not give up its main source of income easily. But if the criminals can be beaten on price, purity and availability, it will leave them largely powerless. How? Governments will have to cooperate. Politicians will need to have unshakable resolve. There will be issues but, in the long term, the benefits for health, well-being, government coffers and society will be enormous.

Recreational drug shops could be like pharmacies, open all-hours and selling drugs manufactured by licensed and regulated factories – just like cigarettes, alcohol and painkillers are today. You would receive advice when you buy them. The drugs would not be contaminated or toxic.

If you want to learn more about the futility of prohibition and the need for a change of thinking, then I would urge you to read two books, written by a man I am very proud to know, Neil Woods, and J. S. Rafaeli. They are called *Good Cop, Bad War* and *Drug Wars*. Neil is a former undercover cop who is now, in my view, the granddaddy of the drug law reform movement. His books make my thinking on the subject look like something hurriedly scribbled on the back of a fag packet and they are compulsory reading for anyone with the slightest interest in how we can change the world for the benefit of all, except the crooks.

22

SUE ME, I DARE YOU

The BBC lawyers were once more troubled when episode eleven of the podcast series was being readied for release. The testimonies of the two former girlfriends were powerful and one of the women had not held back in telling how Parle was violent towards her. The lawyers were quite properly doing their job in considering whether Parle might sue the BBC for alleging that he was a domestic violence offender, when he had never been convicted of any such offences.

Fortunately, they regarded the likelihood of that happening as being very low. If a firm of solicitors wants to write into the BBC next week saying they're representing Kevin Parle and he wants to sue them, then great. That would be a rather big heads-up as to where my quarry has got to. It might then be worth conducting some intrusive surveillance on the solicitors' firm, bugging their phones – and more – in an effort to establish how Parle was communicating with them. I lived in hope.

If the testimonies of the former girlfriends was likely to irritate Parle, then I was sure that another of his former friends was going to have the same effect. He had been in contact with Parle years earlier and told me that his former mate was not always the tough nut, the fearsome character many thought he was today – quite the contrary. This is what the friend had to say:

'I wanted to get in touch. Me and my friends follow the podcast and it was something you said about historical stuff – that what people did in the past may shape their future – that prompted me to get in touch. My mates and Kev's mates all knew each other through Liverpool College but also travelling to watch Liverpool. I've heard you mention that you thought Kev was a member of the Urchins firm [a gang of football hooligans] – well, he was, but perhaps not in the way you'd think.

'Kev loves his cars and driving: it was the one flash thing he loved, so he was happy to hire a minibus to take us to the games. He dressed like a right scruff, but as long as he had some wheels, he was happy. When you told the story of him driving across the farmer's land in the last episode, that really rang true. So, he was an Urchin, but not a hard nut – an Urchin who was the designated driver. He ran with the firm, but Kev in himself is not a hard lad. He's got the size and the front for sure and, if he's confronted, he could shout and scream and exaggerate the Scouse accent and all of that, but he wasn't a fighter.

'I remember we were away at Leicester and one of the undercover policing units – everyone knew them – said to me, "You're Parley's mate, aren't you? He's a tough lad," and I just laughed. A lot of blokes then, if they had something about them in that way, did time on the doors in the city's bars and nightclubs and Kev never did.

'You pointed out that Kev was brought up in Mossley Hill in a nice family. Fighting wasn't in him. If he'd come from Norris Green or Croxteth then maybe, but he didn't. He just wasn't a natural fighter. Hot-headed – yes, definitely. We were at a motorway service station on the way to a match and Kev decided he wanted to impress the young kids on the bus, so he picked up a whole pizza and walked off without paying for it. Sure enough, security came out and he ended up having to pay for it. Hot-headed, yes. Criminal mastermind? No.

'The big cheeses who ran crime wouldn't trust him. They let him run the kids because they looked up to him, but the powers that be saw him as a bit of a clown. I've heard the idea that he was trying to prove himself. When we heard about his alleged involvement in the murders, we were shocked. We thought, If you've done that, that's a big step for you, lad.'

Parle might have changed and become every inch the hard man now – after all, his friend's testimony comes from a long time ago. But if Parle had been listening to that, I wonder if he would have enjoyed being described as a clown? I sincerely hope not.

A woman also contacted me soon after that episode had landed to tell me of a holiday in Spain she had a few years ago. She was standing on the balcony of her apartment one morning, armed with her camera. She intended to take photographs of the view, to take home to show family and friends. Below her on the street she saw a very tall man having an argument with a younger woman. He started to manhandle the woman, looked up and saw my source and the camera in her hand. In a distinguishable Scouse accent, this man shouted abuse and warned her not to take any photos. She was terrified and complied. After seeing photographs in the press and listening to the podcast, this woman is now convinced the man she saw was Kevin Parle. She apologised to me for not taking any photographs of him. I told her not to worry. I didn't blame her in the slightest and just wondered what might have happened to her if she had.

I thought back to the time when I was working undercover in the role of minder to my vastly more experienced colleague who was posing quite brilliantly as an international gangster and businessman. We were in a restaurant meeting some mafioso types. I was not privy to the negotiations because I was 'just' the muscle. A group of ladies were sat at a table near to my colleague and were having a thoroughly enjoyable evening out, when one of them pulled out a camera and started taking photographs.

The camera's field of capture included my 'boss' and the brutes he was having discussions with and there was a possibility that this lady could have inadvertently photographed them – albeit in the background. Regardless, I was across the restaurant in a flash and I snatched the camera from the lady's hand, trying to apologise as I was doing so. The women were shocked into silence as I opened the back, pulled out the roll and exposed the film to the light, thereby destroying any photographs. I stuffed the film in my pocket and handed the camera back to its owner, who was staring at me, open-mouthed. I explained how 'publicity-shy' my boss was and bought them a round of drinks. They weren't the last drinks I bought them but I think I won the group over – eventually. The hoodlums my mate was negotiating with were hugely impressed by my attentiveness and my professionalism. A few days later they were all nicked. If any of the party that was in the restaurant that night is reading this, I'm very sorry. It was all for the greater good.

On a weekend after the release of the latest podcast episode, I had promised my long-suffering wife and two youngest sons that I would dedicate myself to domestic chores, eating with the family and generally giving them my attention. This was in stark contrast to what I'd been doing for most of the year – either boring them rigid about Kevin Parle or working away, hunting him.

The morning started quite promisingly. Under strict and precise instructions I cleaned cupboards and mopped floors until my phone sprung into life, as it so often did. (Between you and me, I was delighted; I've never been the most domesticated type.) My wife begrudgingly excused me from helping and I disappeared upstairs into my office. A brand-new source had reached out to me via a social media messaging platform. Her opening gambit was straight to the point, 'I have seen and met Parle.' Needless to say, this source now had my undivided attention. She wanted cast-iron guarantees that her name would never be disclosed to anyone. That was given. We then went on to exchange message after message. I downloaded and printed off the conversation, which ran to fourteen pages.

I simply hadn't received anything like this before and, although I cannot give you the specifics because my investigation into this information is very much ongoing, I can say that she provided names that I wasn't familiar with, along with dates and locations. I realised immediately that this information would require a huge amount of work in order to develop it fully. This woman was deeply concerned for her own safety, she said: 'If they find out I'm talking to you, I'll end up in the drink with concrete boots on.'

This woman was willing to meet, as was I, but we were in the grip of lockdown as a result of the global pandemic. I kept the conversation going over a couple of days, over which I learnt a lot more. My heart sank when I got a message reading, 'I've said enough. It is not possible for me to speak to you anymore. I have given you a good head-start. Good luck.'

I had to respect the fact that she had decided to call it a day, although the temptation to contact her again has remained strong.

I contacted Kyle. He understood the potential importance of what I had been given and set about his work immediately. Twenty-four hours later, having worked through the night, he got back to me. He had done a remarkable job in extracting every relevant detail from the pages I'd passed to him and had presented his findings in an intelligence document. This was now a treasure trove of intelligence which had come purely from open sources. Much of what my source had told me Kyle had corroborated. Bingo.

Detectives often talk about the 'ABC' of criminal investigations:

A – Accept nothing
B – Believe no one
C – Challenge everything

I applied the formula to the source and her information:

A – I tested as much of the new information as I could while exchanging messages with the source. I also looked into her motives for speaking out. I might have been able to make a better judgement call if we'd had a face-to-face with a real conversation, but that was not to be. Besides, my track record in this regard had anyway been far from perfect.
B – I had believed this source. I'm just a writer with a phone, a pen and a notebook. I don't have access to vast police intelligence databases that might permit more insight into the truthfulness of what I was being told.

C – I challenged what I had heard by sending it to Kyle in its raw form and he had been able to develop and corroborate much of it.

In conclusion, I thought the source was telling the truth, although I had not one shred of evidence - I mean firm evidence, as opposed to corroborating intelligence. And because of lockdown I was confined to my office and was unable to get out on the ground, which I desperately wanted to do.

There was still one more episode of the podcast to go and this new information was so good and so detailed that I decided I was not going to declare any of it, except for a snippet to be used as a cliffhanger. A key part of what I wanted to achieve with the series was to unsettle or irritate Parle, should he be listening, and I was keen to stick with this tactic. There was a method in my madness. Mark and I settled on painting a picture of life under lockdown in the places where we thought Parle could be – Spain, Dubai or Thailand.

For the Spanish element I spoke to my great friend and former *Hunted* deputy, Ben Owen. He was himself trapped in lockdown over there and gave me a great view of life in a country in which lockdown was being enforced very, very strictly. You could only go out to go shopping and the police were stopping and questioning people frequently. The roads in and out of every last village, town and city were blockaded by the police. It was essentially impossible, as Ben saw it, to move around. The rules would apply to Parle, if Spain was his chosen bolthole, at least in theory – I wondered whether he would be tempted to run the risk of breaking lockdown rules and the further and very real risk of standing out from the non-existent crowds. Could something in the podcast unsettle him enough to get him to make a run for it? Mark obtained testimony from Thailand as well as from Dubai, where lockdown was being enforced as strictly as it was in Spain.

I also wanted to conduct a question-and-answer session for what was to be the finale of the first run. Barely a day had gone by when I hadn't been asked about Parle and my hunt – invariably very well thought-out and considered points for discussion. I put out a Twitter plea and got a good response. In spite of all the difficulties and challenges that the fallout from the coronavirus had created, episode twelve was beginning to take shape.

I still had a very big decision to make about the new tranche of information. Should I sit on this intelligence package and do nothing until the lockdown was relaxed? That was very tempting but, in all honesty, it was not really an option. To do so would have been reckless, especially as there was a possibility that Parle could still be living in the place described by the source.

Following discussions with Mark, I called my best mate in the world, Bob. We'd known each other since I'd been a rookie cop back in 1978. He'd had a far more successful police career than me, retiring as a detective inspector after thirty years in the force. He spent the latter years investigating murders and hunting fugitives and still works as an investigator for a government agency. I couldn't have had a wiser or more knowledgeable brain to pick. Deep down, I knew that he was going to tell me what I already knew, but two brains are always better than one. I set up a conference call with Mark, having already sent Bob an anonymised version of the messages with the source. After discussing, analysing and hypothesising at some considerable length, we came to the conclusion, as I knew we would, that I had no choice in the matter. I had to forward this information to the Merseyside DCI.

If Parle was living under strict lockdown rules and still living where we thought he may be, this information could provide the police with a wonderful opportunity to knock on his door. My main fear was that I'd pass the information to the police and then get no feedback whatsoever, based on past experience. I could be left not knowing whether my contribution had been developed or actioned, whether it was of any use at all.

I printed out the conversation thread, cut out or redacted identifying features and rescanned the pages (which, if you're as much of a luddite technophobe as I am, takes an age). I emailed the heavily anonymised intelligence package to the DCI. I said that we were going to pause the podcast but that we planned to be back. I got four words in reply, 'All received. Thank you.'

I needed now to look ahead to when the restrictions affecting everyone were lifted. I started to plan for testing my latest information and moving my investigation forward. I would always give the police the opportunity to say that I shouldn't follow a particular course of action to avoid jeopardising their own inquiries, but I had to prepare to hit the ground running.

I contacted a wonderful friend of mine, another one from my days in uniform back in the 1970s. She had left the police after only a few years and for the last thirty years has had a tremendous career in the commercial security sector. She is incredibly well-connected, vastly experienced and has done me some massive favours in the past. It was her who got me the bodyguarding gig which took me to Dubai. She's a legend in the security industry.

I wanted to sound her out about using some of her intelligence analysts to work on my case. The reply was an instantaneous and resounding 'Yes' - of course it was, she always delivers.

At the time of writing, May 2020, these specialists are poised to do some analytical work for me. They don't come cheap because they are highly trained and incredibly clever people.

We moved towards finalising the last episode of the podcast and the series itself. I was getting the word from former colleagues in London that there was a noticeable drop in more traditional crimes like burglary and robbery because so many people were at home. The police were taking the opportunity to be more proactive in acting against known criminals. Sometimes the doors of targets would disappear off their hinges, while others were getting a more polite knock. Perhaps now the police would have the time to look into long-running cases like that of Parle.

Four days had passed since I gave my new information to the Merseyside DCI. I remembered what an NCA spokesman had said following the arrest of Jamie Acourt in May 2018, 'Our ability to share information and work at speed with our international partners ensures there is no safe haven for fugitives. We will never stop pursuing these individuals.' I reckoned four days was ample time for law enforcement to have taken a look at my intelligence package and to have made a judgement call on whether it had any merit or not. I had yet to hear anything and we were about to wrap up our recording.

We decided to end the episode with a clip from a telephone conversation that I'd had with Kyle. He said, 'I've identified what may be a current address for Parle.' I knew that Parle moved around while he's been on the run. We had proved that. I was convinced he'd been in cahoots with criminals based in one particular area and then moved on to another group of criminals in another location. That would make absolute sense. If the last line of our last episode made him feel so uncomfortable that he felt the need to move, that would also be a very good thing.

Every move Kevin Parle makes increases the likelihood of him encountering law enforcement along the way.

23

CORRUPT OR COCK-UP?

The BBC asked Mark to draw up a budget for future episodes of our podcast series and it looked like we might get another six. These were to be held back until the coronavirus lockdown was lifted sufficiently to enable us to get back on the road. Mark factored in the cost of the two analysts who will work for us. I estimated that we'd need them for three or four days.

The burner phone rang. In fact, I got three calls. The first caller withheld their number and cut me off when I answered. I thought, Here we go, a time-waster – I'm pleased to say I've only had a few of those. Soon afterwards, I spoke to a very decent-sounding guy who didn't want to give his details but told me that he had also known Parle from the days of the Liverpool Urchins, the football firm. He told me much that we already knew, but confirmation is a very good thing and I was very grateful. He did have one story about Parle that I'd not heard before. Around 2004 or 2005, the contact had been in a pub called The Clarence – which apparently no longer exists – and he saw Parle, wearing a three-quarter-length jacket. A mate of the source told him that Parle had a sawn-off shotgun concealed under the garment. The source did not actually see the weapon and I don't have any evidence to support the allegation, but I still thought it was very positive that people were continuing to get in touch.

Not long afterwards the burner phone rang for the third time: 'Is that Peter?'

'Yes,' I replied.

'It's Kevin. I'm hiding in Gibraltar.'

Ho-ho. 'That's nice for you.' Anyway, two can play at taking the piss so I asked, 'Tell me, what's the weather like?' The twat hung up. Why would someone do that? What a waste of time.

The reaction to our final episode was good, in terms of the number of people who came forward as a result. The question-and-answer segment of it had clearly got people thinking and it was one of the most important parts as far as I was concerned: I've always looked at my hunt for Parle as belonging to the people. It will probably be a listener to the podcast or a reader of this book who will come forward with the golden nugget of information that leads to his capture. It is the listeners and readers who keep an eye out while they're sitting on their sunloungers, enjoying a coffee on the terrace of a café.

One of the many questions that came my way was, 'Do you think Kevin Parle is a grass – a police informant – and could that be the reason why he has not been arrested so far?' Well, I've spent some time in the last eighteen months speaking to or being in the company of criminals, one of whom claimed to have been a registered informant for law enforcement. I know from my own experience that informants are sometimes, inappropriately, granted some sort of unofficial immunity, in that their handler may turn a blind eye to their activities as long as information about other criminals continues to flood in. And I am convinced that Parle was not arrested when he should have been …

Back in February 2020, I had been contacted by a man who admitted that he had previously been an informant for the NCA. He was understandably cautious, didn't want to reveal his identity and I have not been able to corroborate his story, although it contained a number of interesting details. About a decade ago, he said, Parle was spending a lot of time on Camping Villamar, the site where I met Graham 'Happy Days' Boland. You will recall that another source had told me that Parle had more recently had influence over people living on that site. My February source was adamant that, around 2009, two plain-clothes officers from British law enforcement were taken onto Villamar by someone who knew Parle well. Apparently, despite the fact that they were in plain clothes, their actions and behaviour made them stick out 'like sore thumbs' as old bill.

These officers apparently entered the bar on Villamar with another person. Parle was at the far end of the bar. He was pointed out to these officers and it was expected that they would then make a dash to arrest him. Not so. Apparently, one of the officers said that they did not have the necessary authority to act on foreign soil and that they would have to liaise with local police. I was told that Parle recognised the covert officers as law enforcement and took the opportunity to promptly disappear from Villamar. I'm told that he then laid low for three months, before feeling confident enough to resurface.

We have to treat this story with some caution because it comes from an anonymous source and remains uncorroborated, but let's just imagine for a moment that every word is true. If it is, then those officers are jobsworths who should hang their heads in shame every day for the rest

of their sorry lives. In my day, wherever I may have been –
be it Tooting or Timbuktu – if I saw a man that I knew was
wanted for two murders, he'd be nicked, end of. I'd deal with
any fallout and take any bollockings that were coming my
way later.

It wouldn't have taken a lot of imagination to circumvent
the legal obstacles. I'd have just arrested Parle straight away
and told the Spanish cops that we'd had a fight and I'd had
to effectively make a citizen's arrest. In all likelihood, that
would have been true because I very much doubt Parle
would have come quietly. I remain absolutely gobsmacked
by this story, and extremely angry. If – and I say again – *if* –
it is true, then those officers are cowards, unworthy of their
jobs, and they have let down a huge number of people. They
are very welcome to contact me and give their side of the
story. Go on, I dare you, and I promise to print every word
you have to say on my website.

This brings me back to the question of whether Parle was,
or indeed still is, a police or security services informant, and
whether or not that accounts for the fact that he has not been
captured. The truth is, I simply don't know. Law enforcement
and the spooks will never tell me. It is just one of a long list
of questions that I shall ask Kevin Parle when he is arrested.

A couple of people posed the question, 'Do you think the
police actually want Kevin Parle caught?' Well, the DCI at
Merseyside has always told me that he and I want the same
thing. I do think, however, it is perfectly reasonable to take
a look at the crimes Parle remains wanted for, the outcomes
from those crimes, and consider whether Merseyside police
or, indeed, the NCA have the appetite to deploy significant
resources to hunting Parle down. Both organisations have
finite resources and enormous workloads.

It's not surprising, of course, that some of the contacts I've made, who are themselves involved in criminality, particularly the ones from Liverpool, hold the Merseyside police in very low regard. It goes beyond 'all coppers are bastards' and into allegations about the force being corrupt as well as incompetent. In my day, corruption was rife and took various forms. There was what was called 'noble cause' corruption, a frankly ludicrous title because there was nothing noble about fabricating evidence or attributing false confessions to prisoners. There was also the other kind of corruption, more about self-interest, by which a team of detectives might seize 10 kilos of cocaine and £100,000 cash, for example and, by the time the suspects had been transferred to the police station, there would be only 5 kilos of cocaine and £50,000 in readies. Those corrupt detectives recycled the drugs into criminal circles for a huge amount of money and enjoyed a very large amount of tax-free cash. Some cops were caught doing exactly that.

Focusing on Parle, I have not one smidgen of evidence to suggest that there is any malpractice in the Merseyside force, but as members of the public ask me the question, it is only right that I discuss it. I've always told my contacts with specific grievances that they can use me as a conduit through which to pass on allegations and they all tend to go rather quiet at that point. Like any police service, Merseyside do not always get it right, but any keen reader of the *Liverpool Echo* will be able to tell you that they frequently do.

If we look at the murder of Liam in 2004, you could argue that the police did a reasonably good job. Anthony Campbell pleaded guilty and got twenty-three years. Other people were convicted of connected offences, relating to assisting Parle. It was not as though Liam's murder was a crime that couldn't be solved, then: quite the contrary. We also know Parle was arrested in the early stages of the inquiry and granted bail. But we also all know what happened then.

If we then fast-forward to Lucy's murder in 2005, which, locally, was a very highly publicised case due to the profile of the victim, the horrific nature of the crime and the associated arson. We know the police arrested and charged Anthony 'Fat Tony' Downes and Kirk Bradley and there was a trial that ended with both men being acquitted. When Parle is found and arrested will the police and the CPS want to revisit Lucy's death? Do they have any new and compelling evidence? Will they be able to even charge Parle with that crime? The original investigation may once again be put under the microscope and could be found wanting. Therefore, the police could attract negative publicity which they would rather do without.

All these matters cut to the question of whether or not Merseyside police have the stomach for arresting Parle and putting him in front of a court. I sincerely hope they do. If they don't, I will have been largely wasting my time. I have not one shred of evidence that would suggest the police don't care about Parle, but I do have questions that they will not answer: how many officers are engaged in the hunt for Parle? What are they actively doing, if anything? How well resourced are these officers?

In my optimistic, perhaps naïve way, I hope the police and the NCA want Parle caught as much as I do. Those questions – is he a grass? Are the police corrupt? – do remain, but the easiest way for law enforcement to answer those is to capture him.

One more question – is Freemasonry still an issue? Masons were around when I was in the police and I saw some ascend to the higher ranks who, quite honestly, had been over-promoted as cadets. I've just finished reading *Undercover Policing and the Corrupt Secret Society Within* by a former undercover detective called Garry Rogers along with Keith Potter. I was quite prepared to lend a quote to the back cover – 'an important book'. It is, for the way in which it details his experiences at the hands of senior cops who were Freemasons in Manchester police. Have the Freemasons anything to do with the Parle case? I just don't know.

The podcast series was over but our esteemed podcast producer Lewis was concerned about a number of negative reviews online. Of course, criticism is part of the process. Any work put out there for public consumption may face attack, but in this case there was a former cop who had been very vocal in slagging me off on social media. He'd made an absolute fool of himself, to be frank, and the public reaction to his derogatory comments showed that his was a lone voice. I know his name and it has been really entertaining to see how upset he gets about me and what he probably perceives to be my success.

I did also consider whether or not the personal comments might have been posted by someone with an interest in Kevin Parle. But I don't think anybody currently harbouring or funding him would be stupid enough to go online and run the risk of leaving a digital footprint. Also, many of the negative reviews used suspiciously similar language and, while I didn't ask Kyle to research them, the similarities stood out a mile. I did think that they came from the same person and I can guess who that is! The former officer I was thinking of was one of those who were always last through the door when we were doing a search, while I always wanted to be first. I'd be the one who would bash in the door and run ahead, shouting,

'Police!' That was my nature. I always had to be at the very heart of the action, whereas this particular sorry excuse for a detective always liked to be at the back, invariably carrying a bag or something and only going in when everything was clear and safe for him to do so.

With the first series of the podcast over, I'm left with begrudging respect for Parle for having managed, successfully, to remain on the run for all these years. And I must extend that respect to those that have helped him because, as I write this now, they are winning. But I'm in this for the long haul and as long as I'm drawing breath and can put one foot in front of the other and have a keyboard to type on, I will not give up.

That is something that the police, the NCA, and anyone assisting Parle should realise. I will not go away. My efforts to drum up publicity will not blow over. Underestimate my determination and my indefatigability at your peril.

24

TALK'S CHEAP

The burner phone rang. A man claimed to have new information about Parle and suggested we should meet. Needless to say, I was up for this, but I wanted to tease whatever I could out of him first.

In an unmistakable Scouse accent, the contact tried to boss the conversation, laying down conditions for the meeting. He told me that I was to travel alone to an extremely remote part of the UK and that I was to meet this man and his brother in a pub situated at the foot of a mountain. I didn't have a problem travelling to a venue of his choice, no matter where it was, but I told him Mark and I operated as a team.

At this point, he deferred to the man he claimed was his brother and I could hear a muffled conversation as he covered the mic with his hand. At length he agreed Mark could come, but added that we were not to bring any recording equipment and said we would be searched. In the decade that I worked undercover I was searched by criminals on a number of occasions. I never conceded without at least a bit of a moan and sometimes I would even kick up quite a stink. Not because I was wearing a wire – I rarely did – but because I thought it showed an unhealthy level of distrust.

On one notable occasion the bad guys made me strip bollock naked, bend over and show them my anus. I consoled myself for a long time afterwards with the fact that they went to jail for many years.

The contact started acting like a complete twat by warning not to bring any police. As if. Mark and I would be followed by his associates to ensure we were alone, he added, as if he thought this would intimidate me. It was obvious that he had not done his homework on me. Time and again he repeated that he had to run things past his brother but when I asked to talk to the other man, he reported that we would only speak face-to-face. I was obviously not in communication with the organ grinder of this operation.

I agreed to his date, time and venue, only to have him call back shortly afterwards. He went off on a rambling rant about how he thought Parle was innocent of both murders. This was a new slant. Apart from the letter that Anthony Downes wrote, no one had raised the issue of guilt or innocence before. These would, anyway, be matters for a court to decide, once Parle's been caught, as I told this contact. He went on to say the date for our meeting would have to be changed and that he would let me know once it had been rescheduled. I allowed him to think he was in charge: it didn't bother me in the slightest that he was trying it on. 'We're bad boys and we'll do it our way.' I'd heard it all in my undercover days. My thinking has always been to let the other side flaunt their attitude if they want – as long as I get to hear what I need to hear, it really is not a problem. He never got back to me.

I was contacted by a man via Facebook who claimed he was a serving police officer working at the Home Office. This was plausible – senior officers work in policy and strategy, updating the Home Secretary on important policing matters.

He didn't give his rank, though, which I thought was odd. I checked his profile on LinkedIn and saw that he had over five hundred contacts, many of whom were also mine. Some of these people I knew and trusted. I thought his approach was genuine but I resolved to proceed with caution.

He told me that he'd been following my Twitter account and the public engagement and he was aware of just how many people out there now really wanted to see Parle captured. I was very glad that Parle being at large was becoming a public interest issue. This officer claimed to have worked on capturing fugitives abroad and to have liaised with forces in the north-west of the UK. He promised me that he was going to 'cut through the politics' and get things done. He didn't elaborate and I was not entirely sure what he meant, but I was optimistic. Parle was now on the radar of an officer working within the Home Office, which was undoubtedly good news. This officer could bring Kevin Parle to the attention of the Home Secretary, who knows? In any event, his approach got me thinking about a plan of my own. It involved a large teapot.

I had been chair of my local cricket club until the end of 2019, having been recruited some years earlier after the previous incumbent had been found with his thieving hands in the till. It was a truly wondrous organisation and a big beast. As a club we played in the region of 350 games each summer, across all age ranges, abilities and sexes. One of the most enjoyable events that the club hosted was a softball festival, featuring clubs from far and wide who descended upon our home ground to take part in an incredibly enjoyable competition. It took an army of volunteers to make the day a success.

At the time of the 2019 festival, Priti Patel was a backbench MP and had a relative taking part who she came to support.

To her credit, the minute she walked into the ground she made a beeline for the kitchen and asked if there was anything she could do to help. I've never said 'No' to any volunteer and in the blink of an eye Priti Patel was on the tea and coffee stall. At the time of writing she is Home Secretary and, if the officer attached to her department does not deliver on his offer of help, I may just have a word in Priti Patel's ear the next time she ventures down to the cricket club. Although, if she's Home Secretary, I suspect I may have to negotiate my way through her entourage of armed police escorts.

By the Easter weekend of 2020, I was very busy. I received an email via an encrypted system from a guy who claimed to have been a police detective in a central European country for nearly twenty years. I'll call him Jan. He said he worked in a computer crime unit for eight years and then formed a fugitive unit where he spent his time hunting, to use his words, 'local, national and international bad guys. We had a lot of successes and lots of failures too'. He went on to explain that he'd left the police because he felt he needed a break, but that he was probably going to go back into the service in the near future. He used a Liam Neeson phrase: 'I have a very particular set of skills.' He told me that he mixed online and field investigations with one purpose only, 'tracking people'. He went on, 'I have a lot of experience in laying traps, for example. So, if I can help, let me know.' Needless to say, I was interested. I'll take all the help I can get.

Jan told me that he thought my push to find Parle was amazing. He said, 'It creates ripple effects that will eventually force the fugitive to make moves, to contact people, to get out of his comfort zone. It may end up with an arrest if the police investigators have wire taps or surveillance. But you need to have a monitoring system already in place to hear the contacts or see the moves or you will have to wait for other people to notify you or for the fugitive to make a mistake.'

I was cautious in my communications with Jan because I'd never met him and, perhaps not surprisingly, I couldn't find anything online. Many cops who work in very sensitive and secretive roles allow absolutely diddly-squat to get on the net. They go to great lengths to ensure that they cannot be traced in any way, shape or form. I decided that I was not going to share any intelligence with Jan until I had been able to confirm exactly who he was. I needed to have him vouched for by somebody I could trust. We agreed to video-call the next day so that I could see his face, his passport and his identifying documents. I always had to be on red alert in case one of Parle's associates disguises themselves, makes an approach and tries to find out what I know.

The following day we had a long conversation via Skype. Jan regaled me tales of very innovative and clever tactics that his fugitive hunting unit had deployed when he was a serving detective. It was of limited immediate use to me as these would have required approval by a very senior police officer or a government minister and, even if I had the resources to deploy them, I would never get such approval. I explained this to Jan, who sounded very disappointed. I pointed out that this was just another example of Parle being able to use his main advantage over me without even trying. He probably disregards many of the laws of any land in which he may live while I do not and will not. It will make his capture all the sweeter.

Jan never got in touch with me again, which I thought was strange, given his initial rush of gushing enthusiasm and willingness to help. I wondered if he was himself a plant, an undercover operative put forward to see if he could entice me into breaking the law. If so, and I had taken the bait,

I could be exposed in the media or have the police come crashing through my door. Either scenario would probably mean that the podcast series would be taken offline. This book would never happen. My hunt for Parle would come to a shuddering halt, which might well please any number of people. If Jan did indeed want to derail my hunt for Kevin Parle he'd have to have got up a bit earlier than he did.

As the weeks ticked by, a considerable number of people kept messaging me with the same question, 'When will *Manhunt* be back?' It was a question that I did not have the answer to. That was in the hands of the scientists, the statisticians and the government as they tackled the coronavirus pandemic. Mark and I discussed strategy in the interim. We had listener loyalty and a brand reputation that we didn't want to jeopardise by diluting the content with filler while lockdown restrictions remained in place. The sound of me bashing a keyboard did not make great podcast material. While we waited for life to get back to normal, I would continue to publicise the podcast on social media and talk about Parle whenever I was asked to do radio commentary on crime and policing, which was quite often. I would also periodically upload short update videos to my website.

The subject of sex workers cropped up yet again in connection with the Kevin Parle hunt. People were asking me what I was doing about engaging with that side of the investigation and one guy suggested that I set up a Facebook page specifically for that purpose. Then, one Saturday evening, a really bizarre thing happened.

I'm now sixty years old. I'm overweight, grey and balding. I am no oil painting. Maybe lockdown cabin fever was coming into play in this story, but as I closed my laptop with a good day's writing behind me, an extremely attractive young lady tweeted a picture of herself, provocatively holding a bottle to her mouth. It gets crazier, a lot crazier. In this tweet, which included my Twitter handle, she said that I was her 'daddy crush' and gave a time and location where she wanted us to meet. Clearly, it was a joke. I looked at this colourful young lady's Twitter profile and it was obvious that she used her sexual prowess to earn money, because she frequently posted extremely raunchy videos that people were urged to subscribe to see. I thought I'd play along with the joke, so I gave her a retweet, meaning that my 24,000 followers would see her approach, together with the line, 'If we were to meet it would be a crushingly disappointing and brief experience for you.'

The following morning I read, 'Have you set off yet?' from a Twitter user. In other words, had I left home to hook up with the sex worker? The nation was in lockdown, I was old enough to be her grandfather and married – this 'meeting' was never going to happen. But I saw an opportunity to have a bit of fun. I noticed that this young lady's account was registered to Manchester and I had been extremely disappointed by the silence following the reveal in episode ten that Michael 'Cazza' Carroll, the notorious Manchester criminal, might be connected with Parle. I had also been disappointed by the lack of response to any of the emails that I had sent to organisations that represent sex workers. Many people had contacted me utterly convinced that Parle would have employed or associated with people who work in the sex industry.

I decided to engage on Twitter with this young woman, pretending that I was making my way for our liaison. I then sent out a series of tweets throughout the day containing jokes about packed lunches, cucumbers, tiny chipolatas, being stopped by the police, and my car getting a flat tyre. All these gags were made at my expense. I was taking the mickey out of myself. To her immense credit this young lady joined in the light-hearted frivolity with responses to my tweets and she clearly had a sense of humour.

I made it very clear that every tweet was completely untrue and included #StayHomeSaveLives, reflecting government advice regarding the coronavirus, with each and every tweet. Anyone who failed to see these interchanges as anything other than a bit of fun obviously had a sense of humour bypass. I released a tweet every hour or so until the appointed time for the encounter, which she had set at 3.30 p.m. At about 4 p.m. I made my last jokey tweet and, as far as I was concerned, concluded the thread. Some Twitter users clearly found it distasteful because they unfollowed me. I suspect this was after they'd looked at her raunchy Twitter account.

Unfortunately, despite our banter, this young lady has not proved to be a gateway to other sex workers. Nor has she disclosed any links or created a pathway for me to contact Carroll. But it was worth a go. It is better to try and fail than not to try at all. This was another example of how I could adopt tactics that the police simply couldn't. This was different. It was innovative. It was worth a go.

I've since discovered that Twitter accounts set up for the sole purpose of distributing porn have enormous user bases, more than 400,000 followers in some cases. If just one of those followers delved into my thread that day, appreciated the humour, followed me and retweeted one of my numerous postings that include flyers of Kevin Parle, who knows where that might lead? I'm willing to try what hasn't been done before.

25

QUESTIONS, QUESTIONS

Another article appeared in the *Liverpool Echo*, courtesy of journalist Luke Traynor, who I have kept in the loop as much as anyone. In return he has regularly written articles about Parle, my hunt for him and the podcast. This piece bore the headline INVESTIGATORS UNCOVER CURRENT ADDRESS FOR DOUBLE-MURDER FUGITIVE KEVIN PARLE, which stemmed from our podcast cliffhanger.

The article stirred up a lot of interest on Twitter, with more likes and retweets than just about any Kevin Parle tweet I'd ever put out there. People were getting very excited. 'Where do you think he is?' Obviously, I wasn't going to tell the public that and thereby tip Parle the wink, and I explained that.

Another user messaged, 'I saw your tweet about having a possible current address for Kevin Parle. I was wondering if this information has been released to the public for tactical reasons. Do you actually have an address or are you just saying you have an address, so he stays on the move and has more chance of messing up? Maybe I just watch too much TV.' Many more questions flooded in. I thought back to the question-and-answer session in the podcast and decided I had better do another one.

I told Mark what I was planning. We'd come a long way from the early days of my hunt, when we'd sit on the quayside in Liverpool having a glass of wine and wondering if anybody else in the world gave a shit about finding Kevin Parle. The podcast had been downloaded some two million times and people were engaging with the hunt all the time. It would come up in the most unexpected circumstances, even as a result of the more light-hearted tweets that I posted as part of my lockdown routine, in an effort to lighten the general mood. As a joke, I'd said that I'd spoken to Father Christmas and he was fine in the lockdown, but that he was asking me to collect wish-lists early. I was amazed when some followers posted that all they wanted for Christmas was to see Parle caught. His capture really was a matter of public interest. I had to turn this to my advantage.

I invited questions from my followers and decided to include the Twitter handles of Merseyside police and the NCA, alongside BBC Sounds and Radio 5 Live. The latter had jointly funded the podcast and I wanted them to be aware of the ongoing interest we had created. As the allotted 10 a.m. slot on a Saturday morning approached, I was ready with eleven questions and the answers which I'd written and saved into drafts. I rang Mark to ask him at what intervals I should post and he suggested every five minutes. At the top of the hour I wished my followers a cheery 'Good morning' and posted the first question. A couple more came in from followers as I was releasing the others and I answered those in real time. This is how it went:

Gaz asked: 'When's the next episode available, Peter?'
'Lockdown means that I cannot travel, knock on doors and get in front of people. However, my hunt

very much continues. We do not want to put out filler episodes, so *Manhunt* has been paused. We'll be back with a cracker.'

Tony asked: 'Peter, I'm all in favour of DNA testing every single child born in this country. In fifteen-to-twenty years' time, any crime committed by any of these people would be found, with the database, almost immediately. What you reckon? Let's start doing it now.'

'This question will get civil libertarians engaged! Personally, I do not want to see newborn babies having their DNA profile harvested and stored on a national database. I do, however, appreciate the potential benefits.'

Andy asked: 'What would you do if you were told coronavirus got to him before you did?'

'If it was proven that Kevin Parle was dead, that may provide some form of closure for the victims' families. But I want proof. I would far rather he was captured alive so he could answer the allegations made against him.'

Kit asked: 'Are there any questions you, on a personal level, want answers to from Kevin Parle?'

'My hunt for Kevin Parle is not personal in any way. Therefore, I have no questions to ask him on that level. However, I'd like to know how he survived on the run for so long in order to help law enforcement in the future.'

Marathon Girl asked: 'Do you feel he is likely to still be trying to move about, which seems to be his habit, despite lockdowns?'

'Kevin Parle has moved around while he has been on the run. However, travel involves a lot of risks. When he has had a secure location with trusted people around him, then he may have remained static for a period of time.'

Stuart asked: 'With his criminal connections, do you think it would be easy for Parle to avoid commercially available travel options and, for instance, get a boat/ small plane to take him from Spain (if he's there) to North Africa or the equivalent, if he's in Thailand or Dubai/Middle East?'

'I'm sure a privately chartered boat or small plane is far preferable to a commercial flight. Check out the escape from the UK of Shane O'Brien.'

James asked: 'What would you do if you came across Parle personally? Obviously, you cannot arrest him and if you call the police, there's a risk of him escaping again. Would you confront him?'

'Kevin Parle is six foot six inches and twenty years younger than me. In a street fight there would only be one winner and it wouldn't be me. I will leave the slapping on of the handcuffs to law enforcement.'

Mike asked: 'Are you concerned that, when you find Parle, the huge publicity about him you have generated may jeopardise the trial and give his barrister a chance to claim this cannot be a fair trial? It would be a crying shame, considering your fantastic efforts.'

'We have often made it clear that Kevin Parle has not been convicted of the crimes he is wanted for. A judge may want a jury selected from people that have not listened to *Manhunt*. We've been very careful about our content.'

Dave asked: 'Do you have any suspects within the Merseyside region who you believe are protecting Parle and possibly know where he is currently located? Those individuals would undoubtedly be looking at long jail sentence unless they assist you and the law enforcement agencies.'

'I have the names of people who are believed to have assisted Kevin Parle while he has been on the run. When he is found, these people may be charged with serious offences. They have a choice – 07908 617694.' [That is my burner phone number.]

Lee asked: 'Thoroughly enjoying *Manhunt*, Peter and Mark. I'm sure you'd love to release more information on the pod than you can, given it's a real-time investigation. How do you balance giving interesting information out in the pod and keeping certain details confidential?'

'There is a balance to be struck. My priority will always be finding him.'

Sam asked: 'From your podcasts it sounds like he mixes with people. Do you think he travels around in a set criminal group or makes friends as he travels with people who don't know his past?'

'I strongly believe Kevin Parle is harboured and assisted by people involved in criminality. Forgive me if I say no more at this stage.'

Andy asked: 'This type of hunt has really gone down well with the public. Do you think there is room to run future series, either by podcast or on TV with multiple hints, like the shows *Hunted* or *Manhunt*? Featuring multiple, real-life targets (I miss *Crimewatch*).'

'I miss the night-time version of *Crimewatch* as well. I think there is room for more podcasts of this nature and maybe a TV show too. A senior detective who is retiring soon wants to join me in hunting fugitives. Let's find Kevin Parle first.'

I signed off, 'Thank you very much for your Kevin Parle questions. Please feel free to keep sending them in. Lockdown does not mean slow-down. *Manhunt* will be back.' I uploaded one of my Kevin Parle flyers and told people that they could contact Merseyside police, the NCA or Crimestoppers if they didn't want to speak to me.

I was very pleased with how it had gone. Some very thoughtful questions had been asked. I learned a long time ago never to underestimate my audience, because the chances were that they would be considerably brighter and better educated than me. The public engagement during the session had been pretty good, I thought. Exactly how good was going to surprise even me.

It pays to advertise. That's what the best detective inspector I ever worked with told me when he was my boss at New Scotland Yard. He insisted that, when we made any significant arrests and when we seized weapons, drugs, counterfeit currencies or stolen goods, we told very senior bosses at the Yard. They in turn would let the media know and that way the public were kept informed of what we were doing, which was absolutely right; it was the public that paid the police's wages and they deserved value for money. It was also a very shrewd move to keep the top brass in the loop.

Twenty-four hours after the question and answer session I accessed Twitter analytics to tally up the number of people who had seen those tweets. I was delighted that there were over 98,000 views of the questions and their answers. I passed the figure on to the DCI at Merseyside and the *Liverpool Echo*. I thought it wouldn't do any harm for them to know about just how many people were showing an interest.

The news that we were suspending the podcast seemed to prompt a number of people to get in touch with me. One man reached out to me via LinkedIn, the managing director of an investigations and intelligence company. We had mutual connections and I spoke to some of them, by way of doing my own due diligence. He had served on the NCA and had earned himself a decent reputation as a very capable operator. So far, so good for this man, who I'll call Nick.

You can't find Nick's company listed on the internet because they simply don't have a website. Most of the small-to-medium-sized investigation companies that are any good don't. Not only do they work in the shadows, but they live in the shadows as well. Finding out about them, and hiring them, is all done by word of mouth. I've often found that the private investigation companies with glitzy websites who shout from the rooftops about how brilliant they are, are very often the exact opposite.

Nick was obviously keen to help because he was in touch with me again very swiftly. We spoke on the phone. He told me that he had members of staff who had time on their hands because of the pandemic and, frankly, they were bored and wanted to help. Kyle was very busy earning a living and trying to locate Michael Carroll. He was also still developing the recent and extremely promising information I had received from my female source. Some extra intelligence-gathering capacity would be very useful, although I still had to exercise caution at all times. I never underestimate Parle and those who harbour him, nor do I lose sight of the fact that there may be some people in law enforcement who might like to compromise the investigation and shut me up.

It became clear that Nick knew his stuff. I was knocked sideways when he thanked me for what I was doing in hunting down Parle. He said he'd listened to and enjoyed the podcast and thought we were doing a really good job.

It's always nice to get a bit of thanks for your work. Talking to Nick made me realise was that there was stuff I hadn't developed as thoroughly as I should.

In my defence, I ask you to remember that I was sitting in the tiny box bedroom of my house, which I grandly call my office. The only person doing this investigation was me. Kyle helped out, Julie helped out, but that was only when I handed information on to them and their other commitments allow them time to work on my stuff. They did the online research and, as vitally important as that was, I was the name and face of the investigation and it was me who people phoned, emailed, contacted via social media and wanted to have meetings with. And so much information has come my way that I have possibly moved on from one piece to another piece without dotting the i's, crossing the t's and going back over stuff as I should have done. Writing this book has also made me realise how much more work there is that I have to do, because I've gone right back to day one of my hunt. Trust me, though, it will get done.

Nick explained very clearly and firmly that I was never going to meet his operatives and that I would never even know their identities; he would be a firewall. I didn't have a problem with that. I was very interested when he told me that some of his team were ex-cops with some experience in the crimes that Parle was wanted for and that they were extremely keen to see him captured.

I had done my due diligence and, while I'd never met Nick face-to-face, I had confirmed who I was speaking to and I was sure he was not a Kevin Parle plant, fed to me so that the fugitive and his cronies could discover what I knew. Nick was the real deal and I decided I'd task him and his staff with developing information from Dubai, because I was still a bit light when it came to understanding how things worked out there. I was very interested to see what they could find out. I wasn't giving them anything current or sensitive. That stuff is always saved for my trusted lieutenant Kyle. Instead, I asked Nick to take a look at Lee Eedle, the man from Liverpool who had been arrested towards the end of 2015 in Dubai, about whom I'd not been able to discover very much. I hadn't put his name in the podcast, but it had cropped up from time to time during my enquiries.

Nick also gave me a bit of a kick up the rear end in terms of what we call operational security. He didn't like the apps that I was using for telephone conversations and he insisted that I switched to a more secure one which I did, happily. He also expressed concern as to whether my other lines of communication had been bugged in some way – my laptop, for example, or my home phone. Those involved in the most serious criminal enterprises make millions upon millions of pounds and can afford to hire crooked private investigators.

Nick's concerns were very reasonable. He told me that he could arrange for someone to come to my house and do a full sweep to ensure that conversations were not being overheard. My house is a bit like Fort Knox in that we've got a state-of-the-art alarm system, CCTV, a steel door that sits in a steel frame, no letterbox and other security measures, so I thought it was highly unlikely that anybody had been able to get into my home to plant some form of listening device. But Nick was also thinking about whether somebody had sent a trojan horse or a keystroke monitor down the line into my laptop. This would mean that every time I hit a key or sent an email it could be monitored remotely. Nick was going to get across all that as soon as lockdown and time would allow. He was very impressive.

We also discussed the possibility of whether law enforcement had bugged my phone. This was first raised by the former Liverpool cop all those months ago. Quite frankly, my answer had been 'No.' You need extremely high-level authority and the target has to be suspected of serious criminality. I remained sure that the police had got far more important things to be getting on with.

The following morning Nick rang me and brought to my attention an Instagram account in the name of Michael Carroll that had the handle Cazza_Salford. This was clearly a spoof account because the biography read, 'Super grassing snitch, me, mate, look at my statements I'm a part-time gangster, full-time snitch, I associate with Leon Cullen and the police.' The feed featured pictures of Carroll, Leon Cullen, a Manchester police badge and an extract from the *Manchester Evening News*, 'Carroll called Salford police on 28 October 2015 and spoke to the detective leading the investigation into the shooting of little Christian Hickey and his mother Jayne two weeks earlier.' Police documents had been posted, headed 'Confidential' and 'Sensitive'; files I suspected had been disclosed to defendants at a previous trial about the shooting of Jayne and Christian.

The person who'd created this Instagram account clearly detested Michael Carroll and the images confirmed what had already been in the press, that Michael Carroll had spoken to the police. I messaged the owner with a link to my podcast and asked them to contact me. I suspected that whoever created that Instagram account was a member of Salford's notorious A Team and might want to do Michael Carroll some pretty serious harm if ever they found him. I had no problem with entering into an unholy alliance, although I would never be a party to anybody exacting retribution.

However, if they had information about Carroll's location, that might assist me in locating Parle, I felt it was only right that I reached out.

I scrolled through the account's followers and looked to see who they were in turn following and was surprised with the significant number of links to people in Liverpool. I know Manchester and Liverpool are not a million miles away from one another, but even so, it was very interesting. I tasked Kyle to do a bit more heavy lifting on researching that front.

I wondered if the police were aware of the account and whether they had pored over it with a fine-tooth comb in an effort to find somebody who may have a link to somebody who may in turn just know the whereabouts of Kevin Parle. I suspected and feared that they probably hadn't, but Kyle would. It was a time-consuming long shot, but one that I felt was worth exploring. I still hoped that the person who set up this account might give me a call, although they haven't yet. I want to talk to Michael Carroll, they want to talk to Michael Carroll (although I fear they probably want to do worse than just talk). The police might never reach out in the way that I have in an effort to set up some kind of dialogue, but that was the benefit of being an investigative writer rather than a cop. I was not constrained by the rules and regulations that so often handcuff our police.

Nick and his team did some cracking background research into Dubai and, while they hadn't found any trace of Carroll or Parle in the Arabic language media, we did talk about how the state controlled the news and the fact that they wouldn't feature stories of the Scouse-scallywags-getting-captured kind. The image of the UAE is that of a safe paradise for all and they were very keen to maintain that front. There had been a newspaper that had inched towards publishing real stories about crime, *7Days*, but that had been closed down in 2016.

Nick told me about Dubai hotels and tower blocks in which you can stay pretty much anonymously. He'd identified residential properties with landlords who didn't even ask tenants for ID. I was getting a greater feel for what might attract a fugitive to Dubai. Nick had also identified a bar that was very popular with people I can best describe as 'shady'.

Finally, I was getting somewhere. The simple fact was that I'd received information indicating Parle could be in Spain, Dubai or Thailand and I'm keeping an open mind with regards to all of them.

26

AN AWARD

Mark, Lewis, Sunetra, the BBC and I had reason for a small celebration. The podcast won an award at the prestigious New York Festivals Radio Awards. We achieved a bronze in the craft category, which essentially was for the sound of the show.

The credit for that award goes to our brilliant producer Lewis, but he was very magnanimous in an email he sent to Mark, Sunetra and me, saying that we had all contributed to the soundscape and the award was recognition of the work we had all put in. I went on Twitter to announce the news and many people responded by saying some lovely things back. I decided to have a beer that night. The stronger and more expensive stuff will have to wait for when the real prize is achieved – the capture of Parle – whenever that may be.

There were other reasons to smile. Worldwide podcast chart listings showed how popular the pod was becoming. We were in the top twenty in countries as diverse as Australia, Finland and Luxembourg, where we were actually No. 1 in the personal journals category. I was very pleased to see that we featured prominently in Thailand. The source who had told us of the unpleasant encounter he had with Parle in Thailand around 2008, contacted me to say he was in lockdown in Bangkok and would be spending his time sending my Thai flyer to his contacts around the country. Interestingly, the podcast charted in the top ten in Spain and in the Philippines, the home of many low-paid Dubai workers.

I had an email from Kyle, which was so often a reason to feel positive. He was making progress on his research into Michael Carroll and had identified what might be an address for him dating back to 2017. I had to remain ever-conscious of the fact that certain sources may try to turn my head towards locations that were manifestly wrong as they try to further protect Parle, but hopefully Kyle's work will help us to tell truth from lies when it came to locations.

Fans of the podcast continued to demand more episodes. What was becoming obvious was that people had a variety of reasons for wanting to see Parle captured. Some were appalled by the murders, rightfully so. Others spoke of their dislike of him and their desire to see him in handcuffs because of his apparent violent and controlling behaviour towards women or even his disregard for the farmer's land and fences, the arrogance of his two-fingered gesture, and the video of his dog dismembering sheep. The podcast had clearly done a very good job in turning many of the listeners firmly against Kevin Parle.

Mark brought an article to my attention in a paper called *Euro Weekly News*, which had such poor grammar and spelling that it appeared to be written by someone whose first language was not English. The headline was along the lines of, FUGITIVE KEVIN PARLE: INVESTIGATORS BELIEVE HE STILL HIDES OUT IN SPAIN FIFTEEN YEARS LATER AS THEY APPEAL FOR INFORMATION TO TRACK HIM DOWN. I strongly suspected that the byline 'George Stephens' was fabricated. Much of the copy had been lifted from other reports, mostly from the *Liverpool Echo*, as far as I could tell, and the article featured a screengrab of me taken from a TV appearance. There were quotes I couldn't remember making, but some of the facts, thankfully, were quite accurate.

I was most interested by a quote at the end of the article, 'One of those private investigators who regularly contacts the *Euro Weekly News* for updates said this morning, "He's elusive for sure, but I have a feeling we will capture him with the assistance of expats living in the Costa Blanca and the Costa del Sol. Even the underworld want him captured for his hideous crimes deemed out of order even by their standards. The hunt will continue until one of us or the police capture him."' My contact details followed, but those words were not mine. I'd never mentioned the Costa del Sol in any media interview, nor in the podcast. That was not the way I talked.

I was fascinated about who might have been indicated by the 'us' – 'one of us or the police capture him'. Were there other private investigators with an interest in Parle? I contacted the newspaper to find 'George Stephens'. There was a hint of a chuckle on the line and I was told this Stephens character was in a meeting. I'm still waiting for him to call back and I shared the article with Twitter, asking again who 'us' might be. I don't have an answer yet, but if there are others out there who are investigating Parle, surely it would make sense if we collaborated?

I marked the first year of the hunt on 29 April 2020. The anniversary seemed to have come around in the blink of an eye. That's what happens when you get to my age – time speeds up. When I was a kid, birthdays used to feel like they took an absolute eternity to reach but now I marked this particular occasion by pausing work on this book to rejig the website. I posted recent articles from the *Liverpool Echo*, among them one with a great headline that screamed, FORMER GIRLFRIENDS DESCRIBE LIFE WITH ALPHA-MALE DOUBLE-MURDER FUGITIVE, with the line beneath, 'One woman claimed he took her on a date with a knife in his trousers.' Another read, LIVERPOOL'S MOST WANTED FUGITIVE STAYED ON COSTA BLANCA HOLIDAY PARK FLASHING THE CASH, the article including the line, 'Kevin Parle had a violent edge, claimed Spain eyewitness.' My particular favourite was, INVESTIGATORS 'UNCOVER CURRENT ADDRESS' FOR DOUBLE-MURDER FUGITIVE KEVIN PARLE, with the article reporting, 'Kevin Parle is now becoming a liability.'

It has always been my intention to transform Kevin Parle from an asset into a liability. I think I'm on the way to achieving that aim. Eventually, I hope that he becomes so well-known that anyone funding or otherwise harbouring him feels that having Parle around is no longer good for business and that they cut him free. All my years as a cop, including a decade working undercover, when I arranged massive drug deals, have made me realise that one of Parle's advantages is that he might be seen, currently anyway, as an asset for those involved in serious and organised crime. Imagine you are stood on a quayside in Europe, negotiating the purchase of a vast shipment of drugs from some villains who have travelled from South America. You turn up accompanied by a bloke who is six-foot six-inches, shaven-headed and built like the proverbial brick shithouse. You have let it be known to the Colombians, Bolivians or Peruvians that your great lump of a minder is wanted in the UK for two murders. He would be a very good deterrent against anybody who may be thinking about stealing your money or suppling sub-standard gear.

I am shrinking the world for Kevin Parle. I am squeezing the planet so tightly that eventually he will pop up somewhere and law enforcement will slap the handcuffs on him. You have contributed to this effort by purchasing and reading this book. Thank you. Please, at the very least, spread the word about him.

I also recorded a short video for the website. I spoke about the anniversary and said that my inquiries were continuing, which was nothing less than the truth. I told the audience that I will be posting regular video updates and thanked everybody for their interest.

I told Twitter and Facebook friends and followers about the video at peterbleksley.com and my website guy was ready to hoover up all the IP addresses of visitors. I had somebody on stand-by to do perfectly legitimate analysis of those addresses, although I didn't think for a moment that Kevin Parle or his cronies would be stupid enough to visit my website from their own laptop connected to their home wifi and thereby potentially give away their location. I was sure if they were tempted to have a look they would disguise their IP addresses by using a virtual private network (VPN) or the dark web. But even finding that someone had hidden their address would be quite revealing in itself and might be something that I would want to pass on to law enforcement, who are always endeavouring to stay one step ahead of the paedophiles, the terrorists and others who abuse the internet for their own nefarious purposes. They might well have the know-how and the expertise to uncover that IP address.

One pleasant upside of being locked down was that I hadn't been trolled or abused for weeks. In fact, I'd received many morale-boosting messages of support and encouragement. Among these, however, was a sobering email:

Hi Peter,
I'm an avid follower of your podcast, *Manhunt: Finding Kevin Parle*.

First, I want to commend you for the work you are doing.

I work in ********** and come across many Liverpool and Manchester criminals. I contact you purely out of concern for your safety. The criminals in Liverpool are on another level and they have no concern for human life. Young kids carry guns and are not scared of pulling the trigger. They are keen to impress their peers, the likes of Parle and other senior figures. I would guess that a price has been put on your head with the work you are doing. Be extremely careful of going to meet any strangers and walking into a trap. I don't want to sound like I'm telling you how to suck eggs with all your experience but my rule for dealing with Scousers is don't trust them. Let's hope for some good news soon.

I remain convinced that a number of people who have given me information about Parle knew more than they were willing to disclose. Was this sender another one of those people? Here's my reply:

I appreciate you taking the time to offer me some wise words regarding my safety. I do all I can to mitigate risk, but the simple truth is that I have made myself a potential target by doing the work that I do. Unscrupulous criminals frighten enough people into falling in line with their perverse thinking, by their campaigns of threats and terror, and I simply will not be cowed. I will not stop until Parle is found or I gasp my last breath, whichever comes soonest.

Should you become privy to any specific plots against me I would very much appreciate a heads up.

EPILOGUE

REFLECT AND GO AGAIN ...

It is the afternoon of 24 May 2020. I have to deliver the manuscript of this book to my publisher today. If the end of 2020 is now looming or has been and gone and you have just read this book then that means only one thing: Kevin Parle has still not been caught. I thank you endlessly for taking an interest in him and my hunt for him. You also pay great testimony to the memories of sixteen-year-old Liam and twenty-two-year-old Lucy.

In writing this book I have had to go back to the very beginning of my hunt and examine my notes, my recordings, my mountain of research documents and more. The fact that Parle is still at large clearly tells how I have so far failed in my quest. I have also come to the harsh realisation through this writing process that I have come up short in many other regards. And that hurts. There are things that I should have done, but haven't. There are people of interest who I should have tracked down, but haven't.

I have compiled a to-do list that is sitting next to my laptop. I have written it in bold, red ink, a glaring reminder of my omissions. In my defence, if I have one, may I remind you that I've largely been operating as a one-man band. Sure,

I've had Mark to drive me, to provide wise counsel and to be a great pal. I've had Kyle to do open-source inquiries and Julie has chipped in. Nick's team did a bit of research for me, but they will be back to their paid work soon. When it comes to being the face, the voice and the investigating team, I've been on my own.

And I've come to a very stark conclusion. Thus far, I've simply not been good enough. I've been naïve to think that I could track down an intelligent, well-connected fugitive like Parle with a notebook, a pen and a mobile phone. If I am to stand any chance of succeeding, I need to raise my game and get some proper help. At first, I wasn't going to declare how much I'd been paid to conduct this hunt but I've changed my mind, so here goes: For this book and the podcast I have so far received eight thousand pounds. Under normal circumstances that would be a significant amount of money, but please bear in mind that I have stayed in hotels for more than six weeks in total, I have made repeated trips to Liverpool and I have also been to Manchester, Warrington, Spain and other places to meet certain sources. I spent a lot of money on one particular source who was not telling the truth. Cars have been hired. A lot of fuel has been burnt. Many trips have been arranged at short notice and I have sometimes had to pay premium fares or rates. Life on the road is expensive when you have to buy every coffee, coke and meal from a café or a restaurant. What I'm telling you, in a long-winded way, is that I've spent every penny on my hunt for Parle. I have not put a single carrot on my family's dinner table.

This is not a sob story. I don't want anyone's sympathy. I'm not skint because I do other work. But all of this has got me thinking about where I go next and I have come to the conclusion that it has to be TV, if I can get a broadcaster interested. I need to employ an open-source intelligence operative who can be adept with social media and has some experience with police investigations. I need that person working with me full-time. Some TV money might just pay their wages for a while.

Many of the sources who have spoken to me about Parle would never want to go on camera. We can work around that. TV might think they are coming into a story that is already part-told and, to an extent, they'd be right, but I'm convinced the launch of this book would be a great starting point. Tomorrow I will start a charm offensive on the broadcasters. Out of loyalty I will go to the BBC first. They backed me and believed in me by commissioning the podcast.

I am utterly convinced that Parle and those who harbour him have considerable resources which quite frankly, I cannot compete with. I desperately need more resources, or to put it bluntly, more cash to pay the experts that will help me find him. I think I've done a half decent job in raising public awareness about Parle, but it's time to up the ante.

Just a short while ago, a contact reported another potential sighting of Parle, on La Palma, Canary Islands. This was around 27 December 2019. I'm getting to that information as soon as I've finished writing this and I will post any updates on my website.

I was contacted by the *Jeremy Vine* show and asked if I would like to take part in their highly regarded series, 'What Makes Us Human?' I could not believe that a bloke like me was being asked to follow in the footsteps of Sir David Attenborough, Stephen Fry and other luminaries who had answered the question. I jumped at the chance, and barely had to think about what I was going to write. I had finished my five-hundred-word essay in next to no time. I make no apology for reproducing it as my final words in this book. It tells you everything you need to know about my motivation to catch Kevin Thomas Parle. I will not rest ...

The Fundamental Rule binds us together. It allows us to go about our business, to enjoy our lives, and it makes us human. What is that rule you may ask? Well, it is basic, it is easy to understand and we abide by it. It simply says, do not kill one another.

In these recent, troubling times, we have seen parliament enact temporary laws that confined us to our homes, prevented the majority of people from going to work and stopped us having family and friends round for a barbeque. Those were mere variations of the fundamental rule.

In normal times – and I'll confess that, as I write this, I don't have the slightest idea what the new 'normal' may look like, but in non-virus, normal times – only 0.001 per cent of people breach the fundamental rule every year. When they do, enormous police resources are dedicated to finding the culprits, to gathering the evidence against them, and to putting the defaulters in front of a court of law. If they are found guilty then they are removed from society, generally speaking, for a very long time, if not for ever.

A tiny number of those who break the rule may find their own lives extinguished courtesy of a police officer's bullet. So be it. Because the rule is the very bedrock of our civilised society, those who break it and seek to spread the fear that the rule will be broken again and again, can expect their punishment to be unforgivingly severe. However, in all other cases, those who break the rule in our great union of countries are not punished with a noose, a fatal injection or an electric chair, because not only do we abide by the rule as individuals, we abide by it as a collective. Our standard default position is that we do not kill our fellow citizens, no matter how seriously or how many times they break the fundamental rule. That is what makes us a flagship nation.

A whole industry of TV drama, films, documentaries, books, podcasts and more thrives on telling us the stories of those who broke the rule. Numerous writers create fictional characters that break the rule, and readers devour their works in enormous quantities. Why this fascination? Because the rule breakers, be they real or make-believe, are not like you and me. They occupy an entirely different world and have a mindset so alien to us that we feel a need to learn about them, their motives and, sadly, their victims.

Unfortunately, an increasing number of offenders are breaking the fundamental rule and getting away with it. Our criminal history books are littered with examples of murderers who have killed once, not been caught and have then gone on to kill again. If you break the rule you simply must be caught because, if not, then we are all in more danger.

This is why my working life is dedicated to researching and writing about those rule-breakers and trying to find them, wherever they may be.

CONTACT THE AUTHOR

If you have any information about Kevin Parle you can contact me via:

07908 617694
peterbleksley@msn.com
🐦 @peterbleksley
📘 Peter Bleksley
📷 peterbleksley
Or message me via my website, www.peterbleksley.com
Alternatively, you can contact Merseyside police via;
www.merseyside.police.uk
Or you can report any information anonymously to
Crimestoppers: 0800 555 111

Thank you.